WISDOM OF LOVE

BREAKTHROUGH WISDOM FOR TRANSFORMING ALL
RELATIONSHIPS INTO DIVINE RELATIONSHIPS

GURU BHANESHWARANAND

BALBOA.PRESS
A DIVISION OF HAY HOUSE

Balboa Press books may be ordered through booksellers or by contacting:

Balboa Press
A Division of Hay House
1663 Liberty Drive
Bloomington, IN 47403
www.balboapress.com
844-682-1282

Print information available on the last page.

ISBN: 978-1-9822-4971-7 (sc)
ISBN: 978-1-9822-4976-2 (e)

Balboa Press rev. date: 08/06/2020

Preamble

IN 2016, I came from India to visit a student of mine in Austria, and upon arriving, one of the first things I noticed was that the people there had a certain sadness about them. I found it unusual that people should be sad in such a beautiful place, and as I was walking through the main street of his hometown, I pointed this out to him. He asked me the reason for this underlying sadness, and we began to observe the pedestrians more closely; we eventually came to the conclusion that only one in ten people looked happy. Everyone else displayed a sadness in their face. I wondered how this could be, and wanted to find out more.

Through meditation and dialogue with Austrians and other Westerners, I discovered that this overall sadness is rooted in unhealthy relationships. I heard about high divorce rates, children growing up hearing their parents argue constantly, and unfulfilled partnerships where love gave way to disappointment, morphing into rejection and hate.

I wondered how this could be remedied; how can I contribute to a positive change? When I flew back to India three weeks later, I knew I had to write a book about relationships. I would explain the natural course of relationships, knowledge which seems strangely absent in Western cultures, and provide insights that would allow people to have better relationships with one another. I believe that the sadness is largely a consequence of children being continually harmed by unhealthy relationships, often culminating in traumatic divorces.

The wisdom shared in this book originates in the Divine Matrix, and is universal. It is a deep truth. The Divine Matrix is an invisible network of energy or consciousness that connects all living beings, both organic and inorganic matter on this earth.

Whoever accesses this energy *can benefit and receive insights and see the bigger picture.* It can be felt as a sudden insight or intuition, and can heal and uplift humanity.

Translating this divine knowledge into human language, and furthermore, from my native Hindi and Sanskrit to English, is a challenge. Nevertheless, I hope to bring you the wisdom I have seen about this topic as truthfully as possible. May the breath of the Universal Divine Matrix touch the readers of this book, and help them transcend their previous ways of thinking into more happiness.

May the readers enjoy the wisdom I can share, and succeed in implementing the newly gained knowledge in their lives and relationships.

Guru Bhaneshwaranand

CHAPTER 1

What Is Love

"Lovers don't finally meet somewhere. They're in each other all along." – Rumi

HOW MUCH OF our life is spent enjoying, suffering from, and dealing with relationships? As social beings, the sharing of our lives with others saturates our experience as much as breathing or eating and even shapes our concept of ourselves to a greater extent than most people realize. The quality of our life depends heavily on the health of our relationships, and it's for this reason that understanding the flow of love which binds our relationships together is so important.

This book explains the natural laws of relationships, the options which each of us are presented with energetically when we are in a relationship, and how we can make healthy decisions to work with love's natural flow. The various forms of love are described, and the various energetic bonds these types of relationships represent in our life are illuminated.

One who understands these mechanisms will be able to more easily navigate the various types of love and relationships and the often treacherous emotional waters they entail. I find it remarkable that the English language has primarily just one word for love. The Inuit people have 30 descriptions for snow, simply because it is crucial to their survival to have an exact description of the element in which they live. If they only had one word for it, they would probably not survive the first winter. It's the same with love; it is equally crucial to our health and survival.

Although everyone talks about it, our ability to describe love in its various forms is limited by its only having one signifier, the word "love." In Sanskrit, by comparison, we have 96 different words for love. Can you imagine a special word for love for the father, one for your partner, your pets, for the sunset, for doubting love, jealous love, unconditional love, and so forth? Our perception and our understanding of love would be so much richer and deeper. The many shades of love coloring our world would expand and open new horizons.

The goal of this book is to provide us with a deeper understanding of love. It explains the common patterns between men and women, fulfilled sexuality, prerequisites of a harmonious partnership, and the possibility of love as a spiritual practice. It is also about the love we have for fathers, mothers, children, friends and even our love of God. Love in all these relationships varies, and to know its intrinsic secrets provides us with unimagined tools to help us master our life in a new way.

The wisdom I convey in this book will allow you to rethink and feel things afresh, with the aim of greater happiness for people in general, and our children in particular, thus providing our future generations with improved conditions for the flourishing of a loving society.

To understand love, we first need to understand that much of what we call love is a total illusion. We'll expand on this in the next chapter.

CHAPTER 2

The Illusion of Love

"Love can be magic. But magic can sometimes just be an illusion." ~Unknown

SPIRITUAL TEACHINGS SPEAK of five great Illusions. Besides fear, hate, shame, and anger, love is also counted among these. Yet how can something so important also be an illusion? What's meant is not that all love is an illusion, but that the illusions we become entangled in when we love in a limited, conditional, interpersonal way are some of the most treacherous, because love itself is such a blissful feeling. It's common for the joyful reality of love to be so wrapped up in illusions that it does us much harm.

The tricky part about romantic love is that it is so beautiful. As long as everything is flowing, it feels like paradise. But when our expectations are not met, we feel we are in hell, which in the most exaggerated circumstances, can lead to very real hellish situations of conflict, mistrust, and despair. The overlooked truth is that love and hate are simply two sides of the same coin in the world of duality in which we exist. However, this is primarily true of conditional, personal love; again, the fact that we have only one word for love becomes problematic.

When we first fall in love romantically, for instance, it's as if our spirit performs a magical dance. Those freshly in love see one another as wonderful beings with magnificent qualities, and everything seems to fit together like never before. Yet, this often briefly glimpsed perfection is an illusion. This kind of love always comes with an expiration date.

To illustrate, let's take the typical arc of a romance based on illusion: A man falls in love with a woman. Enchanted, it seems to him that no woman is better than her, and to her, no man is better than him. They come together and experience the bliss of being in love. Weeks and months go by, maybe years. Their needs for sexuality and physical touch, for closeness, security, and belonging are fulfilled.

Eventually, a new phase begins, and they spend all the facets of their daily life together. In doing so, they inevitably start to see one another's shadow sides, and begin to see each other differently. Being together constantly makes it incredibly difficult, and ultimately impossible for each to hide the unsavory aspects of their personalities, however unconsciously they may have been doing so.

In the fresh moments of new love, this can be incredibly difficult to see. In seeking our happiness through our partner, like a horse wearing blinders, we tend to only see their pleasant aspects, whatever will add to our ecstasy. In time, as the relationship is about to fall apart, our disappointment may may lead us to see the worst in them. The partner may have hardly changed through the course of the relationship, but our perspective of them has taken a 180° turn. We may find ourselves asking, "How could I have been so blind?"

Meanwhile, both sides of each person were there from the beginning, the beautiful and the ugly. When this revelation happens, there is a strong likelihood many will leave the relationship – possibly for a new lover, who they'll only know incompletely again, resulting in a fresh, illusory love to be excited about and eventually become disillusioned with, all over again. Thus the illusion of love continues, for men and women alike, and this is only to touch upon the illusions of romantic love. Family, friendship, and even immature spiritual love all come with their own illusions.

The biggest illusion of all is this kind of limited, time-stamped, intoxicating love. When we are in love, we primarily see the good; when we separate, we see primarily the bad. Meanwhile, the two people have not changed. Knowing this, we should be able to see that both beginning and end are components of one illusion. We actually never saw the truth of the other, but merely what we wanted to see, and eventually what we didn't want to see about them but couldn't avoid.

Part of this is because those in love present themselves in their best light, and not entirely in an intentional way. It's easy to do so, since the partner only wants to see this side of them, and the drunkenness of fresh love brings out only happiness at first. Both more-or-less hide their dark sides, knowingly or unknowingly, and it doesn't help that the other doesn't want to see their darkness, anyway. The underlying reason for this mutual hiding is their fear that the lover will change their mind when they find out the truth, and they often do.

Either partner might later blame the other for knowingly deceiving them, and sometimes that is true. If you approach a relationship wisely, you can anticipate this in advance, but most do not. In a sense, this is just the way we humans are, and so it's unwise to place blame. Even when blinded by the infatuation with the other's courtship dance, we intuitively know whether the partner is a good fit, or not. The trouble is that we may deny this knowing by rationalizing, conforming to socially ingrained ideas, or for many other reasons.

At the very least, when we engage with the other sexually, we all get a sense of whether the relationship will last or not. Each person feels whether they are in tune with the other sexually, and unconsciously perceives the good and bad sides of the partner. In this way, people decide intuitively during the first few weeks whether they want a relationship with a certain partner or not.

If they ignore these intuitions, however, they may enter into an inadvisable relationship in spite of them.

People are not perfect; we all have bright and dark spots, joys and sorrows, hopes and fears. A woman may talk about having met a great man in a new partner, but in reality, she met a good and a bad man in one. When somebody is looking for a person who is only good, they will always be disappointed. Good and bad go together like the gas pedal and brakes. It's not about finding the perfect partner, but loving and accepting them for who they really are. Acceptance and freedom open the doors of love, and lead to a happy and fulfilled life.

He who runs after the goal of finding the right partner will never arrive. He whose goal is to accept the partner as he or she is, opens the door to happiness.

CHAPTER 3

The World of Polarity

"A wise man, recognizing that the world is but an illusion, does not act as if it is real, so he escapes the suffering" ~Buddha

THERE'S A STORY of a Guru who sent two students to the same city on two different missions. The first he asked to find a wholly good person, the other, to find someone who is wholly bad. When they both returned empty-handed a week later, the first student who sought a good person told his Guru, "I found only bad people in the city." The second student who had sought a bad person likewise reported, "In this city, there seem to be only good people."

The Guru nodded, and explained to his students that all we perceive is relative, and so, our experience depends on what we hold within ourselves. The inner attitude with which we approach life's journey generates the seemingly "outer" experiences we have. One way this can manifest is that if we seek an idyllic caricature of either good or bad, we will find only it's opposite, because such perfectly good or bad people do not exist.

Similarly, if someone is sad or depressed, they will perceive the world around them as disturbed and disharmonious. If another feels happy and fulfilled, they will also perceive the world around them as a reflection of that inner state. Though we commonly assume that the outer experience creates the inner feeling, the reverse is true: whatever someone feels inside determines how they see the world.

Our perception of the world around us is a direct reflection of our internal world, and therefore, highly subjective.

This is exactly what happens in the illusion of love, when we unknowingly distort our perceptions of our romantic partners. Based on what is happening within us, our experiences are shaded and warped to such a degree that they barely resemble reality.

When people fall in love, most of them project all their wishes and dreams onto the other person, like a projector casting a picture onto a movie screen. Because of this, what they see in the other person has nothing to do with who that other truly is. The partner simply provides an ideal canvas on which to project our fears and desires, and in fact this is part of what attracts us to them in the first place. Usually, when we believe we are perfect for one another, it is also because our conscious or subconscious shortcomings are a perfect match.

These projections result from desires we have, and the more we desire from our partners, the more we tend to make them responsible for our disappointments, as the relationship inevitably contrasts with our expectations. All of this is difficult to discern during the initial, magical phase of being in love, when we are drunk on infatuation. If we are honest with ourselves, even if only in hindsight, we can recognize that we were not seeing the real person during this time. Behind the glittering facade we project dwells a real human being, with wounds and flaws; we cannot blame them for being who they are, but we can reconsider how we react to them.

Everyone is responsible for how they react to their partner's behavior, and also bears the consequences of their reactions. Each person in a relationship is simply who they are; they have a path of their own, shaped by their life experiences, family history, and ancestors. All of these influences determine how they react to one another, and how they will project onto each other. These reactions often have little to do with the real people behind the mutual projections.

In reality, our reactiveness and conflicts are just the momentary collisions of patterns playing out through us, which are themselves simply echoes of ancient chains of cause and effect; they do not truly belong to us, and are not what we truly are. All of the things we mistakenly think ourselves to be are an endless river of events unfolding through time, and the moment at which they unfold in our relationship is just an eddy in this river. The complexities of these many chains of events culminating momentarily in a conflict are beyond our ability to grasp, but we can at least understand that they are not what we are, because what we are is only Divine Consciousness witnessing this river of limited human experience.

The key is to realize what is happening, and to take a step back from it. As soon as two people recognize the true nature of this situation, how the conflicts arising between them are not truly their own, and no longer make one another responsible for their happiness, the relationship will automatically blossom into something more mature, harmonious, and beautiful. As long as we remain ignorant of the true dynamics of what is happening, we will be hijacked by these patterns. Our power to create better relationships lies in our ability to choose to stop the chain of cause and effect of these unhealthy patterns.

The path away from this mutual projection also requires self-love. This is because we are all ultimately the same, in spite of our superficial differences. As soon as we accept more of our personal characteristics as they are, people and situations we hadn't understood before will become illuminated, and we won't feel compelled to change them. Just as we look with love upon others we care about, we should be able to look upon ourselves with the same love and compassion. Imagine seeing yourself from the perspective of the larger universe, seeing how small and insignificant you really are, how meandering your mistakes, yet all motivated by a semi-conscious search for the spark of Divine Love within you. We are all like that, including your partner, and all the things about them you may want to change.

This futile effort to change people invariably leads to conflict and unhappiness in our relationships. The perfect partner we think we will get by changing the other never comes. Trying to change them is like squirming in quicksand, and can only lead to suffocation.

It is illusionary to think we could change another person. They may or may not change, and may even change in ways we hadn't expected, and don't like. The best thing we can do is to learn to accept each other as we are. This is the true meaning of Love, and opens the way for a harmonious partnership. But how do we accept that which seems perfectly designed to torment us, as relationship conflicts so often do?

Nobody can truly change another. What remains is to change oneself.

CHAPTER 4

Unconditional Love

"You love flowers, but you cut them. You love animals, but you eat them. You tell me you love me, so now I'm scared!" - Anonymous

EVERYONE HAS A deep longing for it, but few even recognize and understand it, and fewer still manage to fully become it. Unconditional Love, self-realized Love, is a type of love that's very different from the love we know. It's a state of being, rather than a feeling. It doesn't lead to hate, disappointment, or loneliness when it isn't reciprocated as expected, since it operates beyond the world of duality. It does not want to help, alter, protect, or own another, because it simply "is." It does not come with expectations, and does not depend on conditions, but rather exists within, unchanged by external circumstances, including our partner's behaviors. For clarity, I will delineate this kind of love with capitalization, "Love."

When we lack understanding, we are busy with the "doing" of love. Then, particularly in relationships, we have reactiveness, sexual attachments, expectations, and conditions we require, in order to love. These naturally entail disappointment, and thus fluctuations in the love we experience, times when we feel we cannot love because expectations weren't met. Only with the transformation from conditional loving to becoming Love itself are these obstacles slowly diffused. Only then can our Love be truly free, to the degree that we can even release relationships when their time has expired without the heartache that is usually involved, because we no longer depend on them.

Since unconditional Love emerges from an internal state of being, it is not directed to a person, or persons. Unconditional Love in the truest sense is not a Love which you have "for" someone else. This is a Love which is self-sufficient, and sets you free. In the context of relationships, it respects and accepts the other, and doesn't validate or judge, because it doesn't depend on the other for anything. It flows from the heart with or without them. It embraces the other exactly as they are, with no conditions.

This Love is eternal and always accessible, because it is actually our true nature, the core of what we are. As long as we are bound by the illusion of duality, the identification with ego and perception of a world of separate objects, it's difficult or even impossible to completely embody this type of Love. We can, however, begin to experience more and more of this Love, and this is greatly assisted by coming into contact with an enlightened person, who embodies it more fully. When we are exposed to such a beacon of Love, we feel assured, safe, and understood. This can help us to learn to tap into this unconditional love within us, which is comparable to connecting to an already existing frequency. This is not like a light switch that is switched from off to on, but is usually a process of awakening by degrees.

Very few living human beings are enlightened or self-realized, which is to say, living in this state of constant unconditional Love. We may have the best intentions to do so, but we always fall short, due to our own entanglements in the illusion of separateness, the inability to directly experience the unity of all. Even when manifested imperfectly, however, having some access to this wellspring of Love within oneself is better than having none at all. Many live their whole lives without even realizing it exists, yet it is present within each person, and learning to set it free can transform our lives.

For most people, it is enough to recognize where our illusions of love limit us, where our essence of Love is restrained by expectations and conditions, and in those moments of recognition, to loosen the reins a bit. Small adjustments towards unconditional Love can move mountains in terms of improving our relationships, bringing more happiness and fulfillment to ourselves and others. While few will reach a state of complete enlightenment, we can all gradually illuminate our lives with more of this unconditional Love, by removing its obstacles within ourselves.

We can also find reflections of this unconditional Love in nature. Trees, flowers, and animals come and go in the course of the seasons. They are born, they die, and new life is created once again. Creation does not stop in the face of death, illness, or natural disasters. No matter how dark a winter, nature always rises in all its might again, in the spring. The young seedling and the old crooked tree exist alongside and even help one another - we are learning - through their complex interconnected root systems.

Nature does not discriminate between right or wrong, ugly or beautiful. All is good, and all is allowed to exist. If only we could accept one another, with all our differences, the way that nature accepts the trees of the forest. When we incorporate and embody this consciousness of allowing, ceasing to judge, and releasing our expectations, we develop the ability to love unconditionally, to love the way that nature loves.

Few people know unconditional Love in its purity, but even small changes towards it can improve our lives and our relationships fundamentally.

CHAPTER 5

The Flow of Love

"Love is a fire. But whether it is going to warm your heart or burn down your house, you can never tell."
~Joan Crawford

ONE OF THE key aspects of living a life with wisdom regarding the dynamics of love is learning how love's flow shifts and takes different forms. Understanding the flow of love is greatly helped by introducing five essential concepts, all revolving around the available quantity of love, the categories of love, and the hierarchy of these different categories. I have decided to outline these points one by one, to make them as clear as possible.

The first rule of love is that there are always exceptions to the rule. Though I speak of types and patterns, please understand that these are general guidelines we can observe. However, love does not belong in a box; it is a living thing, and it may not always play by its own general rules, or always follow the most common patterns.

Love is not just love. There are actually four different types of love, based on different types of relationships: friendly, familial, romantic, and spiritual. These types of love differ from each other in quality. We will further elaborate on each in the next chapter. For now, it's important to just know that there are four, that they have different intensities and qualities, and that within each category, there is a finite amount of love that is available for relationships.

1. Love Is Limited

The first principle to understand is that personal love is limited, but it is only limited within its own category. This means that if our capacity for romantic love is filled, we won't have any more space for additional romantic loves, however, it doesn't necessarily affect our capacity for familial love, friendship love etc. However, when we share all of our love within a specific category with one person, there will be less available for others of the same category.

2. The Hierarchy of Loves

The next important principle is that these four types of love are arranged into a hierarchy. In other words, one has more power than the next, and so on. Depending on whether family, lovers, friends, spiritual teachers, or even God is concerned, there are various gradations as to how intense our love is. In case one of these types of love is put to the test, and you have to choose between one or the other, the one higher up in the hierarchy usually wins. This does not mean that one category is draining the other, however; hierarchy is a separate issue. This will become clearer in the following chapters.

3. Love's Changing Flow

Lastly, the flow of love changes during the course of our life. As a baby, our flow of love is very different than when we're twenty, and then again, at age sixty. This flow is actually what I am describing as "intensity," and so the level of flow or intensity shifts across our lifespans to different individuals in our lives, based on the patterns laid down and determined by nature. Knowing and accepting this natural shifting is a key to alleviating much suffering, and freeing ourselves from various misconceptions we may have about who "should" love who, or how love of any type should last forever.

If we learn about the natural flow of love in different contexts, different times of life, different relationships, things which once caused us much suffering become no longer problematic. After all, would you be jealous of the wind, or bitter that a river doesn't flow where you want it to? In the same way, we can understand how love, to a great extent, is simply a force of nature, which goes where it will. Our attempts to control it, then, are mostly futile. When we live in acceptance, our lives and relationships are happier.

The love we have available to give follows natural laws, independent of any cultural affiliations. Accepting and working with these natural laws is the right way to live a happy life in relationship to others.

CHAPTER 6

Natural Flow in Relationships

"As comfortable as I was with my adoption, the nature-versus-nurture question has been a big one for me. I adore my parents, but I always wondered if I would feel a different kind of love—not more or less, just different—for someone who was biologically related."
~Emily Procter

NEXT, WE'LL DISCUSS the four types of love alluded to earlier. These categories of love pertain to four types of relationships, which in order of priority are:

1. Spiritual relationships
2. Romantic relationships
3. Familial/blood relationships
4. Friendships

I've arranged these according to their significance, which is determined by the intensity of love we feel in those various kinds of bonds. Spiritual relationship is highest, and therefore more intense and significant than the romantic, which is higher than the blood relationship, which in turn is higher than friendship. Again, to make it clear when I am referring to this highest, unconditional, spiritual form of Love, I will use the capital "L."

Each of these types of relationships automatically encapsulates the energy of the types below it. A romantic relationship, for example, includes the energy of the blood relationship and friendship, and the blood relationship includes the energy of friendship. A romantic partner becomes like family, our family usually involves an element of friendship with the relatives, and our relationship to a spiritual teacher involves elements of all of them.

The highest energetic form of relationship is the spiritual, which is a relationship in which unconditional Love, as described in the fourth chapter, flows free of expectations and conditions. This type is very rare. It is a connection with the Divine Source, with God or the Divine, towards which the spiritual teacher guides their students. It can only fully manifest when someone has reached an enlightened state, free of the desire to impose or manipulate, and of the distorted behavior such desire can lead to.

At times, the natural shifting of the flow of love between the various types of relationships can cause confusion or discord, because we don't understand what's happening, nor the reasons for it. This means that understanding it is also the route to freedom from this darkness.

In the coming chapters, we will learn why disharmony arises in the context of the various lower types of relationships. Why do a mother-in-law and daughter-in-law tend to argue, why does the adult son side with his wife, or why will a woman spend more time with a new partner than with her own child. Why do fathers tend to spend less time with their children from their first marriage, once they decide to start a new family.

All these phenomena are based on the natural energy flow in relationships. Some of these behaviors are in direct conflict with the moral codes of society, and may at times cause some of us to initially reject the ideas we are reading in this book. This is especially the case when what's being described directly applies to the reader; it can be far more difficult to see the truth in these teachings when the reader personally identifies with the situations described, so please bear this in mind as you read on.

Romantic relationships are not spiritual relationships, as much as blood relationships are not of a romantic nature. These types of relationships are simultaneously exclusive, yet contain one another in a nested hierarchy.

CHAPTER 7

The Romantic Love Relationship

"Love is like quicksilver in the hand. Leave the fingers open and it stays. Clutch it, and it darts away." – Dorothy Parker

LOVE IN THE context of romantic relationships is usually colored with a myriad of expectations and fantasies, oftentimes going hand-in-hand with wishful thinking, and phantoms of the imagination without any connection to reality. There is no other area of life with as many misconceptions as in romantic love, yet it is also the most potent type of love short of the spiritual.

One of the erroneous beliefs which haunt romantic relationships is the longing for an idealized, fairy-tale prince or princess. When we encounter the desire for the one and only partner who will be altogether different from the other flawed human beings, we are dealing with a deep illusion, which is perpetuated and stuffed down our throats by all types of media. In truth, there are no twin souls or soulmates. Another related illusion is that of an everlasting love, and the belief that our love relationships are based on a deep, eternal spiritual bond.

The intensity of a romantic relationship is determined by three factors. The first factor is the attraction based on external features. That includes appearance, figure, style of clothing, demeanor, and social standing. These factors are influenced by our personal preference, which in turn is shaped by our biology, upbringing, impressions, and life experiences. In common vernacular, we may say that sons marry someone like their mother, and daughters someone like their father.

The second factor is determined by our desire for sexuality. The emotional power of a romantic relationship which sets it apart from friendship or blood relationships happens through the physical and sensual encounter. This is the biggest difference between romantic and these other types of love. Our degree of romantic love is directly related to the quality and intensity of attraction and orgasms experienced with our lover. This second factor is the strongest and most relevant of the three.

The third and weakest factor in love relationships is what I call the "inner click." It is an inherent connection we feel towards someone. This connection can exist due to a past incarnation together, similar current life experiences, or simply shared thought processes. It can also relate to the way a partner mirrors our own psychological makeup, including our shadows. Part of what brings lovers together is how their psychological makeup "resonates" in this way.

All three factors influence our sex hormones, and the resulting pheromone-composition of our bodies, which is detected by the olfactory smell of the other, and processed subconsciously. In short, hormones and the autonomic nervous system, and the resulting emotional reactions, decide largely whether we fall in love or not.

While some might feel this takes the romance out of it, there is some value in becoming disillusioned with the more mechanical aspects of romantic love. It doesn't mean we can't still enjoy them, just that we should be mature enough to recognize that much of what drives our romantic behaviors is actually a sort of hormonal drunkenness, which often involves elements of addiction, as well.

The intensity of a romantic relationship depends on the quality of the sex shared between the partners.

Part of the romantic relationship is the desire to share a life together, to live together. When this desire is not present, we speak only of a sexual encounter. That may be a one-night-stand or an affair, where only the sexual desire is expressed. When a desire for shared life experiences is added to a sexual desire, we speak of romance.

As part of the natural flow of normal romantic love, the physical desire usually wanes around the seventh year of the relationship. That is not a definite number, the dwindling can take place much sooner, or later. Whenever it happens, this reduces or removes the romantic part of the relationship. However, this waning of sexual intensity does not mean that couples need to separate. In many cases, other important factors have developed during the love relationship which provide a promise of continuation.

It may be that a deep friendship and appreciation for each other develops. The birth of one or more children causes a strong family bond, and financial elements can factor into the decision to stay together, as well. There are also couples who, out of fear of loneliness, poverty, or inability to find a new partner, continue the relationship because they feel they have to.

The terrible seventh year exists, because around this time the natural and biological flow of romantic love in a relationship diminishes.

Staying together in spite of this change often leads to a deeper connection. Couples who remain together for 15 years or more have usually weathered many small and large crises, oftentimes leading to the development of a deep trust in one another, and in the relationship. This automatically creates a deeper connection. Even though romantic love has diminished, the relationship can still be deep and meaningful in other ways.

Many couples stay together long after they've passed the period of extinction of sexual lust. The romantic relationship ranks higher than the blood relationship and friendship, but includes the energies of those two types. In this way, partners can become friends, or even like family, and this is often what helps them to stay together past the demise of the sexual bond.

The energetic power of the romantic relationship in comparison to the other, lower types of relationships explains why family members often get the short end of the stick when a couple falls deeply in love, and lesser relationships are put to the test. The same is true for friendships; it's normal that close friends suddenly don't have time for each other, as their romantic relationships take precedence. We have all seen this unfold in our lives, and those of our friends.

When feelings of jealousy emerge due to competition between a romance and a relationship with a close friend, it is friendship that gives way, and rarely the romance. When one or both parents are against the new romantic partner, it is the parents who find themselves alienated by their son or daughter, if he or she is truly in love. Our society does not want to accept these facts, but it is an energetic truth based on the different degrees of love which flow in relationships, and how they become automatically prioritized in our behaviors.

Remember, the love of the romance doesn't take away or drain love from the familial relations or other categories, but the priority of the romance does take precedence. Just because a person will ultimately choose their romantic partner over family approval doesn't mean the partner has taken the love they had for the family, but rather, that it is a more intense category of love.

Once we understand the hierarchical position of romantic relationships to friends and family members, it is much easier to deal with the shifts, and avoid problems and heartache.

Practical Tips for Romantic Partnerships

1. Don't expect anything from your partner.
2. Allow your partner space. Let him or her be free! Try not to possess them or to dictate to them how they should be.
3. Respect your partner's opinion even if you don't agree.
4. Discover mutual interests. Look for things you can share with each other. Be open for each other and for the things you are both interested in.
5. Love the peculiarities and differences in the partner, instead of criticizing them.
6. Don't spend all your time together. When you spend time apart, you will appreciate each other longer, and the romance will last longer.
7. Incorporate principles of tantric sexuality into your relationship.

CHAPTER 8

The Blood Relationship

"Children betrayed their parents by becoming their own people." ~ Leslye Walton

THE BLOOD RELATIONSHIP category begins with the immediate family. Highest among these relationships are usually those between parents and children, as well as between siblings, and even grandparents and grandchildren. Usually lower than these are relationships between half sisters and half brothers, cousins, aunts and uncles, and their nieces and nephews. So, the nearer they are genetically, the more love we generally feel.

Another important factor with blood relations is that the love usually flows from the older to the younger generations, meaning parents often love their younger children more than the older ones. This is another energetic truth that society has a hard time accepting. Convention dictates that all children should receive the same level of attention. This book does not try to dissuade from such a practice, but the tendency to love the younger children more is observable in most family dynamics.

Following the same principle, older siblings may love their younger brothers and sisters more than the other way round. This energetic principle has an evolutionary advantage. When we take a closer look, we can understand how it supports the perpetuation of the species and procreation, as humans, unlike many animals, require enormous care and protection through their developmental years. Therefore, rather than fighting this, it is healthier to see it as evolution providing the most vulnerable and weak with the most affection and protection. While it may seem unfair, it actually isn't, because the younger generally do need it more.

Another example is that adult children rarely care for their aging parents with the same intensity, affection, and self deprivation as they experienced from their parents. This is a sad fact of life from the parents' point of view, but from an evolutionary standpoint the parents are irrelevant, once they have passed their reproductive age. When a child dies the pain is oftentimes unbearable, and may paralyze them for months, if not years. In turn, when a parent dies, it hurts, but not with a fraction of the same intensity.

This is an important component of the evolutionary cycle; since children need the strength of the parents to provide for them, instead of being consumed by the pain of the inevitable death of their parents. One can easily see, with some detachment, how the energetic laws of love are perfectly in harmony with evolutionary needs and their optimal fulfillment.

Energetically, it makes no sense that parents expect to be paid back the energy they once extended to their children, when they were young. The love of the children does not flow back to them, but instead to the next generation. Children share the love they once received to their own children; they "pay it forward," in that sense. Once grandchildren are born, the love that the parents had for their children shifts to their grandchildren. Thus it should come as no surprise when they are more generous to their grandchildren, showering them with gifts and allowing them to be themselves often more-so than they were able to do with their own children.

The flow of energy from old to young allows the younger generations to grow and develop by the wisdom of the elders. Thus, family units and ancestral lineages stay intact. Nature is truly wise in her ways.

The natural flow of love in a family always flows from old to young. Families that understand and surrender to this natural energetic shift more easily avoid unnecessary heartache.

Below is a description of the typical sequence of blood relationship love as experienced by a small child.

1. When a baby is born, it does not experience love at first. At birth, you can take a newborn from its mother and give it to another, and the baby will not feel any lack.
2. After two to three months, this will change, and one hundred percent of the love the baby feels is directed toward the mother.
3. After approximately six months, part of the love is transferred to the father. At age one, about thirty percent of the love goes to the father, and seventy percent to the mother.
4. After about nine months, some of the love also goes to other family members, like grandparents, uncles and aunts, etc.
5. Around age three, another major shift takes place. Some of the love which was previously directed towards the parents is now, step-by-step, transferred to the siblings.
6. By age six the lion's share of the love previously directed towards the parents is towards the siblings.

This process is often painful for parents, due to a lack of understanding of its normality and purpose, but is nevertheless inevitable. If understood and expected from the beginning, much of this pain can be avoided.

I would like to further illustrate this phenomenon with some examples.

Let's assume that two small children are friends, and play together. A stranger comes along and starts to hurt one of the children. It is most likely that the brother or sister, even though they might be physically at a disadvantage, will do everything in their power to stop the intruder. Maybe they'll pick up rocks in order to stone them, or similar. The love is so strong that siblings will often jeopardize their own safety in order to protect each other.

Here's another incident, which I heard about recently. A boy took his parents' car during their absence, and drove it into a pond. Then, he pulled out the car with a tractor, and cleaned up the car in order to cover up the incident, but told his brother about it. Weeks later, the parents noticed the damage, but the brother was determined to take the secret to his grave. Recently, I spoke to the family about the incident, and even after 15 years, the parents still didn't know certain details about it. The brother, who knew all the details, kept them to himself all those years. What I would like to convey here is that at a certain age, loyalty shifts to the siblings, rather than the parents.

The relationship changes once again when the individual in our example has children of their own. This is the point where all or most of the familial love available to a person goes to their own children, and at this point the love for their siblings is reduced to almost zero, unless a person has no children of their own for it to be shifted to. This may not be obvious, but in high-pressure situations, such as perhaps inheritance battles, it will come to the forefront. While siblings maintain a sort of bond, the depth of their love for one another is not the same as when they were younger, and without children of their own.

Furthermore, it's important to note that at the age of about thirty or over, the relationship with siblings will often take a negative turn. This does not mean that siblings older than thirty will not understand each other on a superficial basis, but as soon as the relationship is put to the test, the feelings for each other often turn to hatred. Well known examples are feuds when something is at stake, when siblings work in the same company, or when the inheritance of the parents is at issue.

For people who don't have their own children, part of the love for the siblings stays intact. The love will never be as strong as it was during childhood or teenage years, but will not diminish to the point that it does when siblings have their own children. This can result in the childless sibling feeling that their familial love is not returned in kind by their brothers or sisters who are starting their own families. Once again, understanding that this is simply part of nature can help reduce negative reactions to this situation.

Once this generation has their own children, the love in our example moves again, according to the same patterns. As grandfather and grandmother, the love which thus far was directed toward the children becomes focused on the grandchildren. Based on their life experience and the different positions all now hold in the family unit, it can be observed that grandparents are much more lenient with their grandchildren, spoil them more, and allow them to be themselves, more so than the parents, and more than they themselves were with their children.

Every person has a certain amount of love to give. Where this love flows will change in the course of life, and follows clear energetic rules determined by nature.

The blood relationship is irrevocable. A child can reject its parents and parents can reject their children, but the energetic bond remains forever. This relationship is stronger than friendship, but weaker than the romantic and spiritual relationships. Thus, it can be explained why partners put each other first, and parents second. The energy among a couple is stronger than the bond they feel to their parents, who should not feel rejected as a result. Still, it is part of the nature of relationships that adult children still love and care for their parents, though it's not the same as the stronger natural flow from parent to child, or grandparent to grandchild.

The strength of blood relationship is demonstrated when an adopted child meets their biological parents. It will feel like an invisible bond, a familiarity in spite of never having previously met. Thus, it's easy to create a relationship when biological parents reunite with a child they had given up. Whether it's successful will again depend on various factors, like the age of the child, and the willingness of the biological parents to get involved and take ownership of their parenthood. Naturally, the younger the child is, the more easily the love of the biological parents will redirect to them.

The most important factors to understand in the shifting flow of familial love is that it always tends to flow towards the most genetically similar, and also the youngest members of the family, as inevitably as water flowing downhill. This is why we have the greatest affinity for our children, our grandchildren, our parents, our siblings, etc.

Practical Tips for Family Relationships

1. Accept that love flows from the older to the younger family members. Don't get upset when your children or grandchildren love you less. Once you understand the natural flow of love it will no longer upset you.
2. Recognize the fact that love relationships have a higher rank than familial relationships. That will help you not to get hurt when family members prioritize their romantic partners.
3. Know and accept that siblings go their own way around the age of 30.

CHAPTER 9

Friendship

"A friend is someone who grants you complete freedom to be yourself." ~ Jim Morrison

IT'S SAID THAT there's nothing better than a good friend. Friends are wonderful, they add joy and variety to our lives. Friends can be good advisors, help in difficult situations, and are there for us when we need them. But in the end, friendships have the lowest energetic value of our relationships involving love. Why, then, are friendships considered by some as the highest form of relationship?

The reason is simple. Relationships with a lower energetic bond have less potential for conflict, pain, and injury. Because of the lesser bond, problems are less likely to appear. Thus these relationships are more resilient and will have less ups and downs, which is good, when they serve their purpose, as long as we understand that they won't have the same depth as the other types.

Friendships rank lower than romantic and blood relations, and this is seen when friends' needs are put on the back burner, when we are seriously concerned with our partner, parents, siblings, or grandparents. When put to the test, friendships are less resilient than romantic relationships, and even blood relations. There is an important rule to be remembered, as far as friendships are concerned: If you value your friendship, do not meddle in your friends' romantic relationship.

In very few cases do friendships last a lifetime. Friends accompany one another for certain periods in their lives – during school, college, when the children are young, or as colleagues. Most of us have seen longtime friends move away, and while there may be tears and promises when you say good-bye, at their new location there are new people, colleagues, and neighbors. New friendships are formed and the old fade away. There is the occasional phone call, now and then a visit. But one cannot maintain the same intensity over distance.

Friendships are so valuable precisely because they are at the bottom of the hierarchy. Just because they are less involved emotionally, friends are oftentimes the most valuable advisors, with the least friction between personalities.

We can see the mechanics of friendships when we observe children who move to a new location with their parents. At the beginning, there is lots of drama, because the child has to leave the familiar environment. It hurts, and the separation from their friends can take some time to overcome, but once they arrive at the new home and school, the new surroundings, the children let the old friends fade away, bit-by-bit, and form new bonds.

Then, there are those friendships that last a lifetime. This usually has one of two reasons: either the friends have unusually similar thought patterns, whether from the beginning or by going through much together, or they are different in just such a way that they complement each other. If friends have known one another for many years, or have gone through very unique and significant events together, this can contribute to a so-called similarity bond. On the other hand, there is also a kind of magnetic bond of friendship that can occur when their opposite traits balance one another, and these can also make highly effective "duo" teams for business or various other kinds of projects.

Either way, their similarity or complementarity gives a value to the friendship that can't be matched by new connections. In the case where they are different but complementary, it can appear from the outside not to be very deep, because they are so different, but that can often be a good base for the friendship to last.

The degree of similar thought patterns can indicate the depth of a friendship and how long it will last.

Practical Tips for Friendships

1. Speak at least once a month, especially if you live in different locations.
2. Find mutual interests.
3. Meet as often as possible.
4. When it's time to take a break in the friendship or even bring it to an end, let it go, and leave it open; you never know when you may want to pick it back up again, or simply maintain a more distant friendship.

CHAPTER 10

The Spiritual Relationship

"If you love something, set it free. If it comes back, it is yours. If it doesn't, it never was." —Unknown

THE HIGHEST FORM of Love is the spiritual relationship. It is mentioned last, even though it is ranked first. It represents the highest and strongest form of loving energy. We only mention it last because it is experienced and sought after by only a few human beings, and often only after some dissatisfaction with the other types of love. Once it is experienced, all other relationships are subordinate to it, and are included within it.

At this point, we discuss the relationship to the Divine Source, and whoever might represent or serve as a conduit to that Source for us, be it God or Gods, or the spiritual teacher, who makes him or herself available as a channel for the Divine Source. The Love that emanates from the Source or teacher is unconditional Love, free of expectations and judgments, which causes the same Love to emerge in the pupil, disciple, or devotee.

The spiritual relationship is what helps us find this unconditional Love, to see it as our true nature, and to gradually learn to more effectively embody it and allow it to pour forth from within us. The dynamic of the spiritual relationship is different from that found between partners, siblings, or friends, although it contains all the elements of lower kinds of relationships. When people develop a Love for God in the context of worship and religion, it can at times turn into a spiritual Love, a Love void of expectations, but not always.

When the spiritual relationship takes the form of a connection with a spiritual teacher or enlightened being, we bask in the radiance of Love from him or her. This is a wonderful force that brings great potential for transformation.

The Love that an enlightened person holds inside is a continuous state that does not have the same subject-object relationship as the other types of love. This Love is without aim or direction "at" anyone. It simply is, and emanates naturally from the deepest part of them. Because its obstacles are removed, it exists for all those who are prepared and able to receive it. It encompasses all of the relationships, whether romantic, blood relations, or friendship. It is the Alpha and Omega of Love, and is like a force field that can be felt by all those who come in proximity of it.

Everyone has the ability to obtain unconditional Love, if he or she desires it sufficiently, and is prepared to take the necessary steps and do the work required to embody it. For some people it will be easier, and for others more difficult, but everyone alive can attain this goal.

The true path to Love takes place within us, and requires a change of focus from the external to the internal world. The deeper we immerse ourselves in this process, the more we understand on a deeper and deeper level that nothing exists outside of ourselves. An enlightened teacher can assist us in our travel from the outer to the inner reality, he can facilitate the journey. Along the way, Love becomes more and more unconditional, and external factors lose their grip, until they do not matter anymore. Our love changes step by step from a state of doing to a state of being, as we learn to unleash the endless Love within us.

For those who have known love only in its limited form, coming into contact with unconditional Love through an enlightened teacher is a unique experience. All human beings have a deep desire to be Loved in such a way, to be in the presence of unconditional acceptance. When they are introduced to such a Love and allow themselves to open to it, the unlimited freedom this Love provides also engenders a deep sense of trust. This is the Love which has called the devotees to their Gurus throughout history, and has always served as the catalyst for awakening to occur.

When a person embodies unconditional Love, all those entering their presence experience a resonance, and become more loving in whatever way is possible for each of them. Because this Love is the true nature lying dormant in every person's being, when it is mirrored to them by one who can provide a more perfect reflection of it, it naturally stirs and erupts from the hearts of all who see that reflection. This state of pure Love is so powerful, it even can cause an enemy to let go of their hate, and let it melt into Love.

The lesson of unconditional Love one learns from the spiritual relationship means that we can be at peace with the coming and going of all types of relationships, since we no longer have the false sense of depending on them. When you learn to tap into the ultimate, endless resource of spiritual Love within yourself, you no longer require anything from anyone to experience it, and therefore, are free of all the limitations of normal, finite, relational love. Loving another person transforms from depending on them for love into simply being Love together.

A Guru will help us greatly along this journey, by causing this endless wellspring to gush forth abundantly, and by teaching us how to remove obstacles and free ourselves from the shackles our social upbringing has placed on us.

One knows that their Love is spiritual in nature, when they can let a loved one go without feeling any pain.

CHAPTER 11

Sexuality as Basis for the Romantic Relationship

"Sexual pleasure is, I agree, a passion to which all others are subordinate but in which they all unite." ~ Marquis de Sade

AS WE BRIEFLY discussed in the chapter on romantic relationships, sexuality is the primary factor in romantic love, and what separates it from other types of love. I have witnessed this dynamic with thousands of people, and discussed the matter many times over, and I know how this subject can ignite an outcry in people. I ask those of you who currently experience such internal objections, please don't shut me out right away. I know very well that it is difficult to see past the illusion of what we have mistakenly thought of as love.

The fact remains, it's ultimately not about talking to each other, eating with each other, or living together. It's not even about money, security, or to have someone to help with our problems. All of that is nice, and has its own appeal, but also, all of that can happen in the friendship or familial contexts; in the end, what gives romantic relationships their potency is that we come together in order to have sex, and to live this sexuality with each other, to experience the ecstasy of good sex on a regular basis. If the sex is not good from the beginning, it is an indication that two people are not a good match to lead a satisfying, longlasting relationship, and most of all to start a family with children.

This subject is rather controversial, and so I decided to give it its own chapter. It requires further explanation, perhaps because of the stigma around sex in many cultures. After all, we all love the idea of a loving romantic relationship, which is not only based on sex, but also on higher ideals. Most people want a relationship that is not only romantic in nature, but also provides intellectual stimulation, deep conversation, shared adventures, humor, and togetherness combined with deep understanding for each other. Not to worry, all that is there as well. After all, each romantic relationship also includes all the types of relationships that are below it in the hierarchy.

Still, what keeps the romantic relationship alive is the sex. The better the sex, the more romantic energy exists in the relationship. The bond is created through the sexual energies, which are exchanged physically between partners. Even very good sex that is briefly enjoyed in its quality can create a lasting bond between people, long after the sexual chemistry dries up. This exchange is powerful in its psychological import, and not to be underestimated. A fulfilled sexuality carries us through the ups and downs of daily life, and even many incompatibilities between us. The dark sides of the other are seen as less bothersome, and the togetherness is imbued by the fulfillment of sexual experiences together.

The more a person is not sexually fulfilled, the more the focus on what they do not like in the other will emerge, often without the slightest suspicion of the connection between these two things. This becomes like sand in the engine, which starts the process of separation, and manifests in increasing bickering and arguments. Partners can live like this for many years, without being truly connected. Should the sex disappear one day, it is only a matter of time before the relationship and its energetic status diminishes, whether the couple chooses to stay together for other reasons or not.

The intensity of the sexual experience is in direct proportion to the strength of the romantic bond that is being formed.

The greatest challenge in a healthy romantic relationship lies in the natural dwindling of the sexual desire after six or seven years. Somewhere during this period, the sexual attraction fades, and the bond of the romantic relationship disappears. If one is not prepared for this, the "happily ever after" can turn into a nightmare, because the ignorant and unfounded hope that this need would be fulfilled forever by our partner is shattered.

All of this doesn't mean that you cannot still lead a satisfying and harmonious long term relationship, past the seven-year hurdle. In particular, if one wants to start a family with children, one should take this development into account ahead of time, since children need a 20-year relationship in order to grow up emotionally healthy. Even if the relationship diminishes in its romantic nature, couples can still live harmoniously and even experience satisfying sexuality together.

In order to strengthen the romantic power of the relationship and to maintain a higher level of love, there are two options. The first is variety. Changing our routines periodically is the best medicine. Humans always like something new. If we consciously build this into the relationship, we can maintain the mutual attraction more easily. This can take place in many different ways, from changing the color of the living room walls to joint vacations, or new experimental sexual practices.

The most important and valuable tool to stem the tide of dwindling sexual attraction is the sexual practice and way of life called Tantra. It provides lasting passion and increasing desire for sex, in a seemingly miraculous contradiction of the natural course of things. The practice not only helps the couple to experience a deeper level of sexuality, it also provides a platform to increase love and affection. This is because it begins to make you realize the spiritual nature of the love you experience in your sexual/romantic relationships, for in truth, all kinds of love are shades of spiritual Love.

The most effective way to maintain the romantic power of a relationship is to learn and practice sexual Tantra.

CHAPTER 12

The Tantric Way to a Fulfilled Sexuality

"If a man can possess a woman sexually -really possess-he won't need to control her ideas, her opinions, her clothes, her friends, even her other lovers." ~ Toni Bentley

THE KNOWLEDGE OF this art of love is ancient, but has been lost, and is only recently being rediscovered by modern society over the past few decades. It is up to us to bring it back into our lives, relationships, and culture.

In past times when this knowledge was more widespread, the art of loving created such a depth and closeness between two people, that it was unlikely that they would ever separate. Both couples old and new reach a whole new level in their relationship, through the deep and fulfilling sexual play of Tantra. The sooner they apply it, the better they will feel in their romance.

In order to understand the difference between normal and tantric sex, we first have to understand the functionality of the male and female body. Women and men are physiologically different, in more than just the obvious ways.

Generally, men are easily aroused and can reach an orgasm in a short period of time. Women take more time, and preparation. Due to this difference, the man has often finished before the woman has even reached maximum arousal. If the woman does not reach climax it is viewed as a failure. The man failed her, because he did not bring the woman to an orgasm. Also, the woman may feel guilty. This whole exchange is often seen in terms of performance and results, which produces stress.

This cannot happen with tantric sexuality. The path becomes the goal, the means becomes the end. The goal is not so much to reach an orgasm, it is a matter of expanding into each other, to feel and to enjoy each other. The tantric encounter can take hours, and allows both to reach total fulfillment. It builds slowly, through caressing, kissing, and other methods. It is the art of evoking the intensity of the orgasm, and thus greatly enhancing it. This, in turn, causes a high degree of fulfillment. The type of bliss reached through Tantric sex can hardly be reached through any other practices.

Tantric sex is the art of giving and receiving. Not only is one's own satisfaction the focus, but the satisfaction of our partner. The woman is intent that her man is satisfied, and the man does everything to satisfy the woman. This is tantamount. One takes time to talk about their needs, what they like and require for a beautiful encounter. Both women and men are encouraged to communicate their preferences.

Energetically, two opposing poles meet in the encounter of man and woman. The woman's positive pole is her giving heart, and the negative pole is her receiving uterus. The man's positive pole is his giving phallus, and the negative pole is his receiving heart. The meeting of these two opposites is how male and female blend.

An energetic circuit of love starts to happen when man and woman come together. The woman shares her energy, via her heart, to the heart of the man. The man receives this nourishing energy in his heart, and lets it flow to his phallus. There, he shares his energy with the woman's uterus. She receives it, and lets it flow to her heart. This is how male and female aspects are naturally blended, and a circuit of love is completed between man and woman.

This creates a deep, fulfilling flow of love. The male and female energies of creation intermingle through us, which in Tantra can be used to attain another level of spiritual elevation, a balancing of the personal energies, and internal self. Tantra uses this mingling of energies of the man and woman in the sexual act to promote this ideal state of being.

Physically, the energies are exchanged in the form of bodily fluids. The person who has more energy of a certain kind within themselves lets go of this energy, and the person who has less energy of that kind within, receives the energy. Both merge and become one. The woman's root chakra and the man's heart chakra are activated, because each gives the other the type of energy which they have in excess, leading to an overall balanced state in both.

The exchange of sexual energy is not only deeply satisfying, but combined with the right tools, it may also promote spiritual growth.

This is the natural energetic cycle of love. Tantra is the art of optimizing that cycle, and thereby reaching sexual fulfillment, and even greater spiritual fulfillment. Both partners enter a state of receiving and giving. Position and tempo are determined by the woman, since she needs more time and care. The man surrenders control to her. When both interact in such a way, they will each reach the utmost bliss and fulfillment.

This type of sexual encounter engenders great trust and deep connection, coupled with ultimate satisfaction. Couples who connect in such a way will no longer look for another partner, when the fading of sexual desire begins in the natural course of the relationship. Their bodies start to love each other in a deeper way, which provides an unprecedented bond between them.

Also, male problems of premature ejaculation can be healed, because the tantric act does not necessarily depend on an erect state. Without the pressure to perform, men can regain their sexual power. For a fulfilling relationship with a woman, the opposite is warranted, namely to delay ejaculation as long as possible.

Addiction to pornography is also a rampant problem, mostly among men, which few people want to openly discuss, because of social taboos. Men in modern times have turned to pornography in part due to the fact that they don't typically reach a deep satisfaction with their partner. Sexuality between loving partners leads to deep fulfillment, particularly through Tantric practices. As such, it is nurturing and rejuvenating the cells of the body. Pornography and other substitute sexual acts do not have this effect. If you experience true fulfillment in a partnership, you will no longer feel compelled to watch pornography.

A tantric encounter with a partner you love is better than any other form of sex. This deeply satisfying form of sacred sex balances an excessive desire for increasing or varying sexual encounters, because these are actually misplaced desires for more intense sexuality. The craving for fulfillment by frequent intercourse with the partner is similar, and also goes away. The couple will be satiated and fulfilled with occasional tantric encounters. No lack or craving remains to be replenished constantly, and the partnership becomes peaceful and harmonious.

If you are looking for instructions in Tantric sex, you will find many courses offered. They mostly deal with increasing sensuality and passion. Even though they do not teach true Tantra, couples become happier, and the result is fewer separations. That is the most important outcome. A sexual Tantra course is just the beginning, and if you are looking for more, you can seek an enlightened Tantra teacher to delve more deeply into the art.

The origin of Tantra reaches far beyond sexuality, and is a complete spiritual path to inner peace via meditation, yoga, mantras, and rituals. Sexuality is only a small part in Tantra, and actually not a focal point. It is most effective if you approach it as a complete system. Entering deeply into the world of Tantra means going deep into yourself. However, the sexual component of Tantra is the most effective remedy for sexual dissatisfaction in long-term romantic relationships.

Instructions for Trantric Sex for Couples

There are eight aspects to sexual intercourse, called the "Ashtang Maithua".

1. Smaranam: Thinking of each other
2. Kirtanam: To give each other compliments
3. Keli: Enjoying sexual games, including foreplay
4. Prekshanam: To look each other deep into the eyes, while thinking of a deep unification.
5. Guhya Bhashanam: Intimate conversations about sexuality
6. Sankalpa: Intent to have deep and long lasting sex together
7. Adhyavasaya: Deciding to experience long, very long lasting sex together.
8. Kriyanishpatti: Indulging in slow sex, which can last up to two hours

CHAPTER 13

Energetic Attachments Following Intercourse

"Never sleep with someone whose troubles are worse than your own." ~ Nelson Algren

EVERY TIME WE have intercourse with someone, not only a physical exchange happens, but also an energetic exchange takes place. Not only viruses, bacteria or fungi can be physically exchanged, but also, depending on the condition of the ethereal body of the partner, energetic attributes can be inadvertently shared. A transfer of unhealthy patterns, emotional conflicts, and in some cases, even aspects of mental illnesses can result.

Each sexual encounter leaves an energetic impression. The subtle body of each human is unique and stores information. Even in the physical body some biological researchers speak of a cell memory. A person may not know their great grandfather, but his physical attributes and even some of his more subtle patterns may be embedded in their cell memory. Scientists have, for instance, noted how the experiences of parents can influence their children, such as cases of parents who survived the holocaust passing on traces of their trauma to children. Science is only discovering the tip of the iceberg where the exchange of information among people is concerned.

The energies shared are often emotional in nature. If the

partner is aggressive and charged, we first and foremost absorb those energies. If the partner is optimistic, full of desire, and displays a zest for life, we also absorb those energies. The sharing in itself is unbiased as to whether these are positive or constructive, or negative and destructive energies.

This also means that no matter who the person we have sex with is, however generally positive they may be, we will also absorb a certain amount of negative or destructive energy, even if it's only a small amount. People absorb whatever the partner brings—the negative and positive feelings. At the same time, they also connect to their partner's ancestry and all the happy and sorrowful experiences contained therein.

There exist several scientific models attempting to explain how such a phenomenon may come about. For one, there is the "Mirror Neuron System", which describes the existence of a particular kind of neuron in our brains that we all possess to a greater or lesser degree. The more responsive our mirror neurons are, the more deeply we will empathize with other people's feelings. This concerns particularly those we feel close to. We start feeling their sadness, their pain, their happiness as if it was our own. Another attempt to explain this is via the "Electromagnetic Transmission Theory." It states that the brain and heart of every human being transmit a certain pattern or frequency, so to speak, which then can be picked up and interpreted by other human beings around them. Yet another theory, called "Emotional Contagion," describes the human ability to synchronize moods with other individuals or with groups of people. Even though this theory doesn't give any real clues about why this happens, it leans on the observation that such phenomena exist. For example, one crying infant in a hospital ward can easily set off a wave of crying among the remaining infants.

While scientific evidence about all of this is lacking, the myths and tales of human history are full of examples from all cultures and geographic areas dating back to before the dawn of science. In the more esoteric realms of human experience such phenomena have frequently been described all the way up until today. Some of these archetypal ideas that play a role in nearly all of human mythology are described as follows.

One common mythological theme that is found in various cultures and historical settings concerns a sort of possession by negative entities. Considering the many instances where such phenomena have been described throughout human mythology, some of us might even conclude that such things actually exist, unseen by most and at least for now unable to be explained by science. Many such stories have been told and written, maybe just spurred by imagination and fantasy. There are also ancient teachings that tell us about the existence of nonphysical beings. The teachings of Tantra speak of triple-element beings, while Western religious and other spiritual systems speak of ghosts, angels and other ethereal entities. These are believed not to have a body, but to exist nevertheless. They are believed to consist of air, heat, and space. We humans, when we die, are to transition into such a three-element state, meaning that even though we let go of the earthly substance we can still somehow exist in a form of pure consciousness or energy. There are also teachings that individuals, under certain circumstances, can get possessed by such three-element beings. Supposedly when this happens, changes in personality, emotional illnesses, and even physical illnesses can occur. I leave it to you to decide if such a thing is possible or not but I think it significant to mention here, as some of those teachings particularly claim that during any sexual union, the probability of such a spirit transfer is more likely to happen. Without necessarily taking such information at face value, I believe there is often truth and lessons embedded inside mythology. In my own personal experience the transfer of energies among lovers does definitely pose an intensified exchange way beyond something merely physical and the potential ramifications are very real.

Another mythological tale often described in various cultures deals with the phenomenon of black magic and its potential transfer to other individuals. Black magic is said to involve a systematic installation of foreign energies into a human being, all without that person's knowledge or consent. In the process, certain intentions are to be attached to the person, which then will negatively influence the person's life. The more complex the black magic, the more severe and far reaching supposedly its influence.

A lighter form of this phenomenon is said to be a curse, which is supposedly less systematic, and oftentimes happens in a spurt of anger and rage of one person at another. This form of negative energy is said to be less problematic, but to still cause damage, such as that we do if we yell at and internally curse children, who are much more open and vulnerable than adults.

The energy of black magic supposedly works a bit like an illness. When someone has cancer, for instance, and receives chemotherapy, after the therapy no measurable amount of cancer cells may be detected. Still, somewhere, a few of those cells may remain hidden. These cells start dividing again, and after a few years the cancer is back. Black magic is said to work in a similar way. Unlike cancer, however, during sexual intercourse with someone who is affected by black magic, small amounts of this particular energy may be transferred. In time, this transferrence may multiply and grow, until it causes severe physical and emotional symptoms in the person it was passed on to.

Again I am leaving it to you to decide how much of this sounds viable. It is not my point to make any claims about the veracity of such stories; it is rather to show that humans throughout time have always been dealing with such phenomena and have found different explanations for them.

Maybe if we combine those stories with the right amount of science and logic, we will be able to make our own conclusions and maybe even draw valuable lessons from them.

Short of an exact explanation as to the why, I have learned from my personal experience dealing with hundreds of individuals seeking my help, that just like any physical illness can be transferred via bodily fluids from one person to another, so can emotional afflictions somehow make that transfer. And even though we might not quite understand the reasons and pathways for these energetic transfers yet, they do exist. This may also be in part a forgotten reason why, in many ancient societies, monogamous traditions like marriage existed. This at least would have kept many of these negative energies "quarantined" in a sense.

By the way, just like sexual illnesses can be avoided through the use of condoms, so can energetic transfers, for the most part. The use of a condom, however, has a huge disadvantage. Since the physical and energetic exchange of bodily fluids is avoided, so too is the sexual unification on an energetic level. As far as Tantra is concerned, sex with a condom has a greatly reduced significance as a sexual act, compared to the "full contact" alternative. The energetic connection is not fully made.

This explanation should not be interpreted as encouragment to engage in unprotected sex, nor a teaching that prescribes monogamy. These are simply energetic observations that each adult has to evaluate and come to their own conclusions about. They do, however, reveal some of the advantages of monogamy.

In a similar way, healers and those being healed can take on negative energies from each other. Presumably, there are many ways to receive negative energies. Sexual unification is a particular opening, which on the one hand can cause an intensely positive energetic exchange between lovers, but on the other hand, can also be damaging, since we cannot control what is being exchanged. The exchange of energies between partners too often happens haphazardly, meaning all positive as well as negative qualities are exchanged and transferred.

I believe that intercourse is much more than just a physical encounter. Whoever is able to manage well the energies they receive is able to have several sex partners and live in polyamory. For people who have difficulty managing these energies, it is easier to live with only one partner. Whether someone lives monogamously or polyamorously is strictly a personal decision, depending on that person's. Independent of social norms and judgments, there is no better or worse lifestyle as far as monogamy or polyamory are concerned; however, each comes with its own challenges.

Whatever sexual dynamic you choose, a good rule of thumb is: don't have sex with anybody who you wouldn't want to be like.

CHAPTER 14

Women and Men

"I think there's something to the old saying that women use sex to get love, and men use love to get sex. ~ Oliver Markus

IN THIS AND the following chapters, I will be speaking about the differences between men and women in general. It's important to understand that there are exceptions, and I acknowledge this. However, the existence of exceptions does not mean that general patterns don't exist. It's these general patterns which are vital for most couples to understand and about which I speak.

In the Tantric understanding, creation brought forth female and male energies, in the course of the evolutionary process. These energies are represented in roughly a 3:2 ratio in men, and 2:3 ratio in women. Accordingly, men tend to have about one-third more masculine energy, and women have one-third more feminine energy.

The existence of more male energy in men makes them more active, goal-oriented, and protective; in women, the existence of more female energy makes them more passive, nurturing, loving, and open to receiving. This diversity makes them attractive to each other, and helps them find each other, love each other, and bear children. So it is that creation is preserved.

As emotional beings, men and women are essentially equal. Both genders have the same feelings of joy, sorrow, fear, and anger. Their chakras, the energy centers in our bodies, are equally configured and positioned, but with opposite polarity. In men, the root chakra has a positive charge, in women, negative. The polarity of the chakras changes from chakra to chakra, so that, when men and women come together, the energetic polarities complement each other and a strong flow of energy ensues.

Physically, men and women differ due to the hormones, testosterone and estrogen, which exist in different quantities in males and females. Men have more testosterone than women, and women have more estrogen than men. Such disparity causes men and women to feel, think, and act differently and to express their feelings either more directly or less directly.

This can be observed by looking at jealousy. Both men and women get jealous; the difference lies in their expression. Men tend to fight for the woman, by being aggressive with a challenger, or even fighting them. Women will most likely try to solve the problem through less direct methods. They might put the partner under emotional pressure by crying, blaming him, or reacting in other emotionally evocative ways. Alternatively, they may also do everything in their power to make the man feel comfortable in their presence so that he will voluntarily stay with them. Either way, they are less likely to address the issue directly, until it's absolutely unavoidable.

The differences between the genders are partly due to our cultural upbringing, as well. We still often experience gender-specific treatment at home, and to some extent, in the school system. While it might make sense to raise boys and girls differently, too often this is done in unintentionally harmful ways, such as pressuring boys to repress their emotions or making girls believe they should not speak their minds or make their own decisions.

On the flip side, many believe there should be no difference whatsoever in how we raise boys or girls. They may even deny that there are any inherent differences beyond the obvious anatomical ones. Paradoxically, many also believe that someone's bodily anatomy can be out of sync with their internal gender, and must be changed. They can even hold these two contradictory beliefs simultaneously.

In fact, some cultures are caught up in a state of conflicting opinions and ideas about gender and the sexes, which in some ways merely adds another layer of confusion and difficulty to our modern relationships. How shall we sort through it all? How can we understand our biological and psychological differences, without automatically imposing certain ways of being on others?

CHAPTER 15

Female and Male Energies and Devaluation of the Genders

"We may add that it is not an act of justice but of foolish injustice to pretend the sexes are the same. Justice is exercised in respectfully providing for the due needs of each." ~ J. Budziszewski

BEYOND DUALITY, THE reality is that every human being is simply a human being. A woman is a human being. A man is a human being. Though apparently different, as soon as they unite, they meld into one being, a family, a community, a country, a world. The whole universe is a global village in which human beings could live in peace and harmony, if they could just stop focusing on their differences.

Both genders long for peace and harmony but frequently fall short of it due to problems arising from their apparent differences. It's important to remember that the soul has no gender; it merely becomes gendered when it enters into a body and the cultural context that defines that body psychologically. Therefore, all the issues we face culturally around the topic of gender are merely in this domain where the biological meets the psychological. They have little to nothing to do with the soul.

When we see things through the veil of duality, people start to divide society and look for differences. They start to point out qualities like race, skin color, poor vs. rich, citizen vs. foreigner, and woman vs. man. It's not so much that these differences don't exist objectively in some sense, but the problem comes when we use them in order to find our place, to put ourselves higher or lower, to control, determine, and rule, or submit to rule. Judging others provides people with a sense of security and righteousness and a way to feel superior in their way of life. This is one of the primary ways a being living in duality tends to look for a sense of stability.

Each religion declares itself to be the only truth. Each society declares its own principles to be the best. Groups of all kinds often show no interest in what those unlike them may contribute by way of ideas and knowledge, and they often show no interest in reflecting on themselves. This is a common human trait; we care mostly about ourselves and those like us.

The phenomenon of suppression of women by men is oftentimes viewed as a gender-specific issue, but in truth, it is not. This problem is based on power dynamics and the fact that it is the nature of human beings to exploit and suppress others. Exploitation of the powerless by the powerful is built into our society; it is the inevitable result of a world full of people lost in their egos.

Men and women each use their power to elevate themselves, and to look down on the other. Men have always used their physical strength to exploit and abuse girls and women. Women have exploited their roles to more indirectly manipulate and betray boys and men. This abuse of power does not only take place between couples or friends. Older siblings abuse their position towards younger ones. Mothers and fathers sometimes abuse their daughters and sons emotionally, or even physically. This behavior is not gender specific, but rather, the power dynamics among the genders are subsets of a much larger phenomenon.

The tendency to separate, degrade, and exploit is based on fear and concerns our society as a whole. It is the fear of not having enough, not being enough, of losing control, of being unable to love or be loved. In order to resolve this division and restore balance, children should grow up free of fear, with the knowledge that all human beings on this Earth are equal, irrespective of their gender, their origin, or their religion. This way, we can learn to respect and support each other, and peace can be restored in families, society, and the nations of the world.

CHAPTER 16

Men and Women in Modern Society

"The polarity of the sexes is disappearing, and with it erotic love, which is based on this polarity. Men and women become the same, not equals as opposite poles." ~ Erich Fromm

AT THIS POINT, we continue to tread into politically treacherous waters. For many people, even discussing qualities attributed to gender or the sexes is inherently controversial. Still, we would be fools to deny that the differing roles of men and women in the evolution of our species has had no effect on us. These effects mostly pertain to our bodies and their instinctive parts, which are still very relevant to our lives and relationships, especially when it comes to sex and romantic relationships.

While we are, in some ways, transcending the inherent biases of our biology, this doesn't mean we need to deny them. Therefore, please understand that what follows is a generalized discussion of these evolutionary patterns and is not meant to tell anyone what they can or cannot be or do, as the soul is ultimately free and genderless. Understanding sexual differences is simply a matter of gaining knowledge of the bodily vehicles in which our souls travel.

Some of the greatest misunderstandings today pertain to

women and their struggle against male domination in modern societies. Unfortunately, this has led to a great amnesia about what women truly are and the power of the feminine.

To begin with, women are inherently more inclined to be spiritual than men are. This is because they hold the greatest power that a human being can have: they can allow life to be created within themselves, can give birth and nurture. This ability to create a new life is godlike. Spirituality means being able to surrender a certain inner resistance, to accept things the way they are, and to give up our expectations of life. Women have an easier time doing this, since they are naturally equipped with the gift of creation. Surrender and allowing come naturally to them, as in the case of a mother lovingly allowing her children to consume what energy she has to give in caring for them.

The inherent wisdom of this gift and the innate role womanhood plays in evolution has not been considered much in the fight for equal rights. Feminism fought for the equality of men and women in society, and still does, too often with men as the benchmark. Women, by putting themselves on the same level as men, actually lowered themselves, negating the inherent gift of the feminine nature.

At some point in time, someone started the idea that women are weaker than men, even though this was never the case. Women were always simply different in their strengths, and their ability to create life and to nurture bears immense power and a unique position. The first mistake was for some men to view this ability as a weakness; the second was for some women to believe it.

Based on a lack of understanding this, women in Western cultures have assumed they need to be like men in order to take their place in modern society. They have learned to fight and work like men and have forgotten what intrinsic strength lies within them and what value their power of creation holds. This does not negate the obvious truth that women should have equal rights in society, such as the right to vote or equal pay. To abandon the natural gifts of femininity in an attempt to be exactly like men, however, is a mistake.

Men, too, have forgotten their own intrinsic gifts and strengths. Many men no longer know what it means to take care of a woman, to lead the way, and to make decisions with the wellbeing of the woman and family in mind. They have not only lost the knowledge of the power of the female, but, with that, they have also lost access to and trust in their own male power. In many ways, these losses on the part of both men and women are casualties in the war against the idea of gender, a war that is rooted in a fundamental lack of understanding of the wisdom of nature's patterns.

This dichotomy between our inner nature and social values has led to conflicts in relationships. Women try and often succeed in displaying strength and independence while inwardly longing for a strong partner whom they can trust, who will allow them to relax and surrender. Some deep part of them still desires a man who values them, takes them into his arms, and takes care of them so that they may relax and feel good.

This surrender is often mistaken for weakness, but, in reality, it's a strength. It actually takes tremendous power over oneself to surrender, and this act opens the way for positive change to flow. Furthermore, to whom or what she surrenders herself is up to the woman. In this way, surrender can paradoxically be a kind of power. For most women, the only route to feeling well and fulfilled is by being with a strong man who will protect her and her family, and who leads with their wellbeing in mind. This is not the case for every woman, but for most it is. It is the feminine role in romantic relationships.

Women also have a natural desire for a man who is, in one way or another, "superior" to them, another controversial tendency, which is exemplified by a woman's tendency to look for a man in a higher social position than herself and a man's tendency to look for a woman in a lower social position than himself. This may be expressed in the fact that the man is older and has more life experience, that he has more influence, more money, or is smarter. Although this will likely cause many people to bristle, the reasons behind it will be discussed in the coming chapter about women's feminine nature.

A woman desires a man who can direct and lead her.

Conversely, men desire a devoted woman, which allows them to feel strong and relax, not fearing competition. For this reason, a man naturally seeks a woman who looks up to him. He looks for someone who, in his own view, is somewhat below him. This can be expressed in various ways. Maybe he feels he is a bit smarter, more successful, or in some way more competent. A doctor may marry a nurse, the boss his secretary, a musician in a band, one of the band's fans, etc.

A man desires a woman who wants to surrender to him.

This question of the differences between masculine and feminine should not be associated with the question of prohibiting people in general from living as they please. Every man or woman has the choice to be as they see fit. We are only talking about energetic realities, which allow us to live in a state of happiness organically, even though it might not be in line with modern viewpoints. It also doesn't mean that you have to accept these views, just because you are reading about it. You can obviously take from this what you will.

Nevertheless, based on these natural laws, it is an uphill battle for strong women and weak men to find partners. They have fewer partners to choose from, who are weaker or stronger, respectively. It happens that people come together without fulfilling these above-mentioned requirements, but it will be harder for them to lead a happy relationship. It is like swimming upstream in uncharted waters, in many ways, though it is certainly not impossible.

In fact, it happens more and more today that these facts of our existence are rejected, and even forgotten. Instead of valuing these natural differences between men and women, they are considered problems that need to be solved. The conflicts that ensue also affect the area of sexuality. Love can only flourish where partners do well with each other, where they exist in a deeply relaxed state, and both respect their differences. That is the foundation for a truly fulfilling encounter, where sexuality can grow and unfold according to its very old evolutionary patterns.

A woman's devotion is not weakness. She decides who she devotes herself to, and withdraws as soon as her devotion is disrespected or abused.

CHAPTER 17

The Nature of Man

"Manliness consists not in bluff, bravado or loneliness. It consists in daring to do the right thing and facing consequences whether it is in matters social, political or other. It consists in deeds, not words." ~Mahatma Gandhi

THE MAN SEEKS to lead in the relationship. However, leadership skills have to be acquired first, and are often misunderstood. In some cases, this misconception and lack of skill is expressed in being overly controlling, or by relinquishing responsibility, out of resignation, fear of failure, or for other reasons. Most men have never learned to lead out of their inner strength, which is a quality women yearn for. When the man fulfills this yearning in the woman, the man feels fulfilled, as well.

To lead wisely does not mean to control, but to trust. Strictly speaking, it means to surrender control, but maintain certain boundaries. In the traditional role as the head of a family, a man should lead like a benevolent king, who provides others the opportunity to develop their potential, and to lead themselves.

Men's role in evolution has almost always been as the defender of the tribe, who "holds space", who maintains an atmosphere of safety and trust, within which the business of family and community may take place. His natural job is not to micromanage what happens within his "territory", but to maintain outer boundaries of safety and stability, and inner boundaries of acceptable behavior.

A man who is a successful head of a family is not a boss or manager, who wants to rule or give orders, or dispute the execution of each task. He is not only concerned with himself, but seeks to take care of his wife, his family, and his community. He tries to understand their needs and to solve their problems, and most of all to maintain safety and harmony. When he succeeds, it makes him and all those under his care happier.

When he succeeds in helping his family members to live and grow in the shelter of his strength, he lives in his power as a man. As a result of this effort, he receives fulfillment. When the children and the wife make their own decisions, it does not rattle his cage. A man wants to be like the sun that shines and warms all, regardless of the weather.

Wise leadership does not mean to control others, but to trust the partner, to accept her as she is, and simultaneously to take responsibility for her.

CHAPTER 18

The Nature of Woman

"When the power comes from within us and we claim it as our own, then we no longer have to affirm ourselves by dominating others. The irony is that we are actually afraid of our own power." ~ Marion Woodman

MANY WOMEN TODAY face a plight in which they operate within, and are expected to prefer a social milieu that does not correspond to their nature, which leads to great effort and stress. As with men, they have forgotten the true strengths and value of their natural femininity, and why it is fine or even wonderful to be different from men, to have different strengths and gifts.

This is all because of a historical debacle, in which we lost our wisdom and defined women in a way that viewed them as weaker and subordinate, because of their being physically weaker. The result is that women therefore underwent a justified cultural struggle for equality, but many of the reactionary attempts to equal the scales have resulted in distorted perceptions of the genders.

The biggest error is the belief that feminine qualities are weak, because they don't conform to the ideal of masculine strength. Anyone with spiritual wisdom knows that the cradle of power lies in the female, and not in the male aspect of the person. Within each person, whether that person be male or female, the masculine energy is the physically-oriented part, and the feminine is the spiritually-oriented.

Women, through their inherent spirituality and nurturing nature, are in a way superior to men. We can observe this in everyday life. When a small child falls down, it will first run to the mother. It is primarily the mother who will get up at night to care for the children when they are sick. The waiting rooms of pediatricians are primarily filled with mothers, not with fathers. Women generally provide a good atmosphere at work, put flowers on the table, and care for their environment in a more loving way. If you look at it this way, men, by comparison, can be seen as typically lacking in the areas where women are strongest.

Another source of great confusion about the nature of women is a mismatch between modern ideas of equality, and aspects of women's sexual nature. What we too often fail to understand is that, while much of our modern lives transcend biology, our sexual and therefore romantic patterns are still largely determined by nature. This is most easily observed by the "ticking of the biological clock" which women must face, and their desire to raise children potentially disrupting or slowing down their career. Another area where women's desire for equality contradicts their biological patterns is in the instinctual desire to date or marry "up," or in other words, to pair with a man who they perceive as having a higher standing than their own, in some way.

This is a very deep pattern, designed by nature to improve the species, since the woman is the gatekeeper, which decides whose DNA is deserving of continuation through her. This is why women may be very discriminating about their partners, but men are happy to have sex with a majority of women. Nature has designed men to hedge their bets, and women to invest carefully, since they carry a much greater burden of risk, in their biological imperative for childbearing and childrearing.

Yet, in an age when supposing that any man might be superior to any woman is considered blasphemous, this instinctual need to mate "up" becomes problematic, and therefore repressed. If there is no understanding of the purpose of this mechanism, it's easy to see why women would prefer not to think that they are seeking betterment through a man. However, if seen simply as nature attempting to make better children through the woman's choice, it makes perfect sense.

There is nothing inherently wrong with this. It is the nature of a man to be the protector, and provider. He will look for a partner who will allow him to feel strong and protective. Yet, even this sort of thing has become controversial, with many people believing that such cases are inherently victimizing for the woman, simply by virtue of the powerful man being in a higher position to them. Sometimes, men do exploit this asymmetrical power dynamic to coerce, but much of the time it is simply natural, when both parties are happy and consenting.

It's all a part of women's natural role as the gatekeeper and guardian of the process of creation which occurs through them. We may not like the idea that we are instruments of nature's processes, whatever our gender, but life is much easier when we surrender to it, and simply accept these aspects of ourselves. These bodies and their instinctual processes are a "package deal," you can't have one without the other, or at least it's very difficult and serves no great purpose to wage an uphill battle against them.

Women's search for a "high status" man is not a sign of their weakness, but of their power, the power of a gatekeeper, protecting the sacred temple of creation which nature has entrusted to her.

Once such a man is found, then comes the woman's power of surrendering, and allowing, when they feel they can trust that this man will take care of their needs, and keep them safe. One of the greatest blunders of the "war of the sexes" was for men and women both to view surrender and yielding to be a weakness.

There is a wise saying that the yielding, pliant tree survives the storm, while the stiff tree is broken by the wind.

In reality, great things can be accomplished by yielding and allowing, rather than forcing and resisting, and it actually requires great inner strength to do so; it is the strength to set aside your temptation to resist, trusting that most problems have a way of resolving themselves. A passage from the Chinese book of wisdom, the Tao Te Ching, describes a great ruler as one who "doing nothing, accomplishes all things."

These are all expressions of the mysterious wisdom of feminine power that have been all but lost to the modern dialogue of gender and equal rights. Feminine power is expressed by wise people because it doesn't take any wisdom to see male power; men are physically strong, and therefore obviously have brute force on their side. The power of the feminine is subtler, and therefore more easily overlooked. It is a tragedy that we have lost this wisdom.

When we all recognize the inherent feminine strengths, women can stop fighting for the right to mimic men.

In raising children, too, women's gift of allowing shines. Research has shown that positive rather than negative reinforcement, as well as unconditional nurturing support tends to produce healthier adults, all of which are feminine qualities, even in cases where they may be given by men as well. To become vibrant, intelligent, creative people, children need the freedom to express and explore, and too much heavy-handed masculine energy can disrupt this, by setting too many boundaries, trapping them into certain codes of behavior, withering their ability to think for themselves. It is rather the balance of these two which is necessary, which requires the feminine principle.

Of course, women's greater emotional intelligence and connection is also a tremendous gift. Even if children generally prefer their father, when in doubt, most of them will usually team up with their mother, since they usually have a stronger heart connection with her. Men have a harder time developing this aspect, it is a lesser part of the male energy. Men may be good leaders for society in some areas, but as leaders of the heart, women are undisputed. In this way, they are the true leaders - even today.

CHAPTER 19

Separation in Modern Society

"A relationship is like a house. When a light bulb burns out you do not go and buy a new house, you fix the light bulb."- Bernajoy Vaal

AS YOU OBSERVE people in public, you will find that few look happy. This general unhappiness, especially in places which have the greatest material standard of living in the world, points to a broken society. There are some cultural differences in how much people focus on happiness and interpersonal connections. Nordic and Germanic cultures, for instance, are known for being more introverted and serious, while cultures of the global South tend much more towards collectivism and extroversion. Even these differences are not enough to explain the phenomenon, however.

Many marriages end in divorce after 6 - 15 years. Roughly 28% of children in the U.S. live in single-parent households, meaning that about every fourth child does not grow up with both parents. In 2018, 25% percent of people in America have experienced a parent's divorce before turning 18. This doesn't even include the many couples who never married, but have children together, and then split up. Statistics in other developed nations where standard of living is quite high are similar.

Why is it, that those who have the most comfortable life have such a difficult time maintaining the most fundamental structures of society, the family?

Part of the explanation is that the expectations regarding a partnership are higher. Infidelity, debt, stress, alcohol and drug abuse, domestic violence, lack of sex, or general drifting apart are no longer tolerated and endured. This may be due to a culture which is centered more around individualism, rather than social cohesion. What we miss in our individualism is the degree to which we need a stable social environment to be happy, usually more-so than having our personal desires fulfilled. It is certainly what our children need more of.

The statistics, however, do not account for the two main and deeper reasons why parents separate: unfulfilled sexuality and restriction of freedom through controlling behaviors.

When a relationship breaks up, it leaves a scar in our psyche. Old wounds are exposed: "I trusted, was hurt, and betrayed. I must be very cautious about trusting again." The fear of loneliness and abandonment increases, and there is great uncertainty as to how to cope with a life by yourself, to be a single parent, to maintain a relationship with your children, as well as financial stability for them.

All of this can lead to latent depression, which, as far as the children are concerned, means that the parents are not present, since they are busy with their own wounds. At worst, they can even take revenge on the former partner by setting the children against them, demeaning them in front of the child, or by comparing the child with the other parent to scold them. All of these are extremely damaging and unhealthy behaviors resulting from the chaos of divorce.

With every broken relationship, the trust in relationships in general is reduced, in both the parents as well as the children. We don't forget, and as soon as we enter a new relationship, the memory comes back. It is difficult to trust the new partner, since our trust has been violated. This can make genuine human connection next to impossible, and can start a downward spiral of relationships being broken time and time again.

Every problem that exists in today's relationships has existed before. The difference is that now the wellbeing of the children has a lower priority in the decision to stay together. The aspect of the relationship pertaining to raising children, caring and providing for them with a stable environment, has lost its significance for men and women alike. This is the result of inflated egos in general, and a greater emphasis on individual fulfillment.

The likelihood that a relationship will break up is much higher when we ourselves went through a divorce in our own childhood. We will tend to be unhappy because we're no longer able to create a deep connection and trust with a partner. The increase in divorce rates is an indicator of this dilemma, nuclear and even extended families fall apart more and more, generation by generation.

Even the larger social networks of family, friends, and neighbors suffer from the situation. Society is weakened to its core. Social policy measures are meant to counter this trend, but aren't always effective. Traumatized people who are incapable of trust suffer from depression, narcissism, dependency, unemployment, poverty, violence, and crime. Yet few people correctly attribute these problems to the lack of human connection caused by the breakdown of the most fundamental social unit, the family.

It's not too late. We have to be aware and alert as to what is happening, and look for ways to reverse this trend, so future generations can enjoy more balanced and harmonious lives.

CHAPTER 20

Children

"Behind every young child who believes in himself is a parent who believed first." — Matthew Jacobson

RAISING CHILDREN IS one of the most important things we do, culturally, because how they are raised will determine to a large extent the adult they will eventually become. This means that we should put tremendous thought into how we raise our children, and follow natural patterns as much as possible. If we do a good job of raising wise and loving children, we'll soon find ourselves in a more harmonious and happy world.

The optimal timing for childbearing is wholly determined by nature. Humans are animals; we are also more than animals, but our reproductive cycles are subject to biological determination more than most other aspects. Women start their period during their teenage years, and at age 20, are at their prime as far as reproductive potential is concerned. The same is true for men. The genetic quality of the man's semen and the woman's egg is at its peak at that age, and so is the ability to love their children, and care for them. This ability decreases with time, and at about the age of 35, is greatly diminished. Parents in their twenties usually have the most love for their children, though there are exceptions.

At the age of twenty, nine out of ten eggs can turn into a healthy baby. At the age of thirty-eight, it is only one in ten.

I personally would not recommend having the first child after the age of 35, for genetic reasons on the one hand, and for energetic reasons on the other. Older parents have less energy for physical engagement with the children, and additionally, tend to spoil them more, as well. This is not to say older people can never make good parents, but in general, the 20s are "prime time," so to speak.

The parents' natural intensity of love for their children is higher in their twenties than in their thirties, and decreases steadily after that.

CHAPTER 21

The Impact of Divorce on Children

"I am a divorced child, of divided, uncertain background. Within this division I - supposed fruit of their love - no longer exist. It happened nearly forty years ago, yet to me nothing is sadder than my parents' divorce." ~ *Sylvia Kristel*

THE COLLATERAL DAMAGE of adults' focus on their own desires and unwillingness to sacrifice for the family are not a pretty thing for many people to see. It can be a very difficult wake-up call for those who either have divorced, or consider it a possibility. Nevertheless, for children whose parents are separated, the safety net of their childhood is irrevocably broken. They lose their innate trust in love, life, and relationships. This trauma remains during their lifetime, and can only be remedied by therapeutic and/or spiritual work. They are more likely to get divorced themselves, once they are adults, than couples who experienced intact families. Thus, the trauma of separation is passed on to the next generation.

The suffering of children affected by divorce is the root of many trust issues by the ensuing generations.

Children from divorced families rarely realize the full

potential they were born with. It affects their decision-making abilities, and their ability to let a decision mature in their mind. It simply creates more psychological obstacles for them, and makes their lives more difficult.

Children from divorced families are more susceptible to drug abuse and eating disorders, alcoholism, prescription dependency, gambling, media dependency, or becoming workaholics.

Oftentimes, they turn to drugs to help them forget the sadness they experienced in their childhood. The need to avoid those feelings can be so overwhelming that they cannot resist their addictions. They hurt themselves in many ways, and are not able to stop this behavior, no matter how much they try. It's a vicious circle. Even if they don't succumb to drugs, they carry a deep sadness within them that stays with them for the rest of their lives.

The way this pain expresses itself in children, and later in adults, varies. Girls may be more likely to withdraw and act accommodating. Boys may express their pain and try to stand out by their aggressive behavior. As much as girls don't explicitly demonstrate their pain, it is no less severe than with boys. Both suffer from the separation, but often display their suffering in different ways. Of course, the way a divorce actually plays out will be individual and complex, but there is never a separation which has no effect on the child.

The parents' potentially negative behavior before and after the separation only makes things worse. Early in the separation, children experience arguing parents and a subdued, desperate, and aggressive mood in the household. Through intense arguments, the parents lose the respect and reverence of their children and force them to realize that their parents are flawed and broken people at a much earlier age than they should. That can be quite traumatic, since by nature they love and look up to their parents.

This leads many children to decide not to get married or

commit later in life, even if the parents stayed together in spite of not being happy in the marriage. This is why conflict in the home, when it cannot be avoided, should at the very least be hidden from the children.

After the separation, the children have to deal with the parents, who are often left scarred from the process of separation. The parents are so busy with their feelings of pain, anger, and grief that they aren't able to be present with their children. They try to function and manage life - make a living, parenting their children, having hobbies, and making friends, but the sadness and despair is present as an underlying mood. Maybe they will look for another partner, but to enter a new relationship becomes more and more difficult with each separation. It's next to impossible to trust the same way again.

If you want your children to respect you, you need to treat your partner with acceptance and care in front of them, without exceptions.

Consciously or unconsciously, parents know that through the separation, they will cause irrevocable damage to their children. They feel guilty and wish that their child would release them of their guilt. They are afraid that the child will no longer love them, because they have inflicted this pain on them. So, they will often wrestle for their love by putting down the other parent, whether verbally or only inwardly, which will nevertheless unknowingly express itself in subtler ways.

This disparagement of one parent by the other, which oftentimes starts long before the actual separation, is torture for the child. The child suffers, because it feels that it should take the side of one or the other parent, while only wishing that both parents would be back together, in peace.

Children who experienced a divorce will try to bring their parents back together, even many years after the event, and often feel responsible and guilty, when they are not successful. They take on roles and patterns which they carry for the rest of their lives, that will hamper their expression, and will make it difficult to approach a partner sincerely. In other words, they lose a part of themselves.

Out of this deep insecurity and the fear of loss, loneliness, and abandonment, they will become possessive and controlling in their relationships. They tend to be more needy, and cling to and burden the partner with demands. This behavior causes a relationship to become stiff and inflexible. It stifles growth and vitality.

This is typically expressed differently in the genders. Women will often have a hard time trusting men, since they lack the experience of a father who protects her, encourages her, and is by her side. This father figure is something they look for in their partner. Out of fear of losing this man-father, they elevate their partner, while simultaneously trying to put him down and control him. Because of this inner dichotomy they are unable to be fully involved.

Men, on the other hand, often find it difficult to carry out their role as the responsible partner and father. They need qualities like honesty, protectiveness of the woman and family, and fearlessness. These qualities are needed, in order to lead a harmonious partnership as a man. Boys who experienced a separation often lack the trust in these attributes of their masculine power. This causes them to avoid relationships and to take responsibility. They might even hold the belief that partnerships in general don't last anyway, or that they themselves are not capable of a long-term relationship.

In order to grow up in a healthy way, children need an environment of male and female energies. They need love, trust, security, acceptance, support, and appreciation. They need a father that purveys security, assures, and protects them, as well as a mother who feeds and nurtures them. They also need grandparents, who envelop them with their love.

The first step to making a change in society, is to understand that children need these above mentioned benefits, and that it creates collective damage when we don't give them the priority they deserve.

When children lack a parent, then grandparents are the next best solution to bring the missing male or female energy into their life, and to surround them with love. In dealing with our children as a couple, it is important that we learn step-by-step to accept each other with our positive and negative sides. The path is difficult, but it's worth embarking upon today. We have to become aware of our own needs and expectations, so that we can incrementally stop making our partner responsible for our fulfillment.

Just as important for a successful partnership is to engage in mindful sexuality, and utilize knowledge of natural laws regarding relationships. With a better understanding of these things, we can stop the separation spiral that is largely responsible for many of the disturbances in our society. How many relationships have ended in traumatic divorces, simply because of people's inability to understand or communicate their sexual needs? Fixing this problem should be a primary concern in restoring the family unit, which is founded upon sexual attraction and reproduction.

All of these considerations are important, but magnified when children are involved, when we are reproducing and raising a family together. In a childless partnership, there is no inherent problem when one is unable to live in harmony and bliss with their partner. When they become aware of this, they can simply choose not to have children and maybe even to leave the relationship. When we separate as a childless couple, we are the only party involved in the pain, and no children are harmed. The stakes are much lower.

Children are divine creations. They are innocent. It is the

parents' and society's responsibility to guard them. It is not necessarily about making sacrifices, but making the right decisions and living up to the consequences, so that children can grow up in a harmonious environment, and develop their potential. The health of our entire society depends on this, it is the axis on which humanity turns, and we have forgotten it's importance.

In order to grow up in a healthy and balanced fashion, children need male energy from the father, and female energy from the mother.

It might be difficult to accept, as may be other points made in this book, but growing up in a homosexual family comes with a number of drawbacks. Growing up with two mothers or two fathers is a problem in itself, though children may exhibit the differing masculine/feminine qualities regardless of their gender. I have to advise any homosexual couple to seriously reconsider having or adopting children, as difficult as this advice might be to accept. We have to understand that having children shouldn't necessarily be seen in terms of being a "right" the same as voting or getting married. The primary concern should not be about the ability to do whatever heterosexual people are able to do, but the critical importance of the balance of male and female energy for the psychological health of the child.

Another issue for homosexuals raising children is that at least one of the parents is not a biological parent. This means that the energetic connection of the child with that parent and vice versa is missing. In such a case neither the child nor that parent are able to receive the same quality of love as is the case with a biological parent-child relationship. None of this is to say that it's impossible to raise a healthy child in a homosexual family, but simply that it comes with certain drawbacks.

The genetic issue can also appear in heterosexual relationsips, in which children are adopted. It is of course wonderful to be able to provide a home for an orphan, but one has to understand that raising children that are not your genetic offspring requires extra effort to compensate for this lack of genetic connection. In the case of an orphan, it may be better to have a pair of adoptive heterosexual or even homosexual parents, and the balance of energy that brings, than to simply live in an orphanage. On the other hand, if a homosexual couple chooses to raise a child, they may never be able to provide it with the masculine/feminine balance that is ideal.

So, you see, there are many things to consider when it comes to bringing up healthy children. This is not to say that exceptional cases of children raised in non-traditional households will always be a disaster. Humans are resilient, and can thrive in many conditions, especially when love is present. There are successful and healthy children raised by loving single parents, adopted parents, and increasingly, even homosexual parents. These successful cases are because these non-traditional parents take extra care in raising the children; it is harder, but not impossible.

These situations by and large do come with inherent obstacles which we should be aware of in our choices, and we should know that the tried and true balance of masculine and feminine in a healthy heterosexual household is the most preferable environment for raising children. It is what we should strive for, and we should not be under the illusion that it's all the same, and therefore doesn't matter.

CHAPTER 22

Breaking the Cycle of Separation

"All the couples therapy and communication seminars in the world won't save you if you aren't prepared to close your eyes and hug the mainmast through a storm." ~Ada Calhoun

THERE IS NO one perfect prescription in relationships - each couple has to follow their own path. One difficulty is that partners approach the relationship in different ways. Again, we are talking in general here, and in the following paragraphs attempting to explain certain tendencies. That does not mean that these ideas apply one hundred percent to every man and woman.

One of the most important factors in breaking the cycle of separation is simply understanding and anticipating one another's needs and preferences. One would think this might come naturally, but for various reasons, men and women seem to perpetually misunderstand one another, and therefore a conscious effort must be made.

One area this misunderstanding frequently plays out lies in differing needs for physical intimacy. Often, women will like to cuddle frequently, while men may tend not to enjoy much touching, outside of sexual encounters. In some cases, the genders may be reversed in this dynamic, but a difference in desire for physical intimacy is something to be aware of. Even when it comes to sex, women often like to be touched all over their body and breasts before the man makes sexual contact with her vulva. Men like it when the woman touches their sexual organs immediately, and require very little foreplay.

Another difference is the closeness versus distance ratio of the sexes. Men prefer to switch between short lived closeness and distance. They need distance, in order to engage again. Women go through cycles of wanting constant closeness, which helps make their love get deeper and stronger. This love builds slowly until it climaxes, and then withdraws, in order to build again. This slow rising and falling wave pattern can be observed in women's patterns of intimacy.

During periods of stress, men tend to retreat and deflect, while women usually want to process their experiences verbally. Women generally like to talk more in the relationship. They like to discuss their various needs and look for solutions for their problems in order to keep the relationship alive. Men often-times feel that it is better not to talk too much about it, that most problems will naturally be resolved without explicitly addressing them. The difficulty is the mutual judgment in this regard. Women judge men's silence as lack of interest, and men think that women doubt the relationship when they talk so much about relationship concerns.

When the difference in desire for communication is not understood by either party, this is another area that can lead to serious problems. Let's say a man has a job where he needs to speak a lot, such as a salesman. When he comes home, he probably doesn't want to talk any more, his "talking energy" has been spent. The woman, on the other hand, may have an almost inexhaustible source of the same talkative energy, and may demand communication from him. This is incompatible with his nature, and his specific needs in that moment.

Another very important area is sexual attractiveness. Both

sexes experience sexual attraction to traits in the opposite sex which are mostly determined by nature, and are very different. It's important for each gender to understand these common patterns of instinctive attraction, in order to cultivate healthy relationships, as well as avoid wasting our energy fighting against nature. We should all have a basic understanding of what is required to be sexually attractive to the opposite sex in general, as well as to our individual partner.

In general, men's attraction to women is simpler, and more physiological. Basically, men are programmed to be aroused by physical indicators of biological health and youthful vitality, because nature has designed them to seek the most fertile and healthy females of our species to mate with. Physical fitness, skin quality, and general energy levels are all indicators of this. Secondary factors may include qualities of femininity, nurturing, and other more personal preferences.

Women, on the other hand, tend to be attracted to subtler indicators of worthwhile genes. Nature, in her "lazy" genius of always taking the path of least resistance, simply outsourced this more complex assessment to the community as a whole. Therefore, the primary factor in most women's attraction on an instinctive level is the esteem a man has within his community. This is why you see so many women fawning over whichever men are socially regarded as important, especially when they are younger, and more driven by their instincts.

These could be leaders, bosses, performers, politicians, professors, doctors, or even just popular men with excellent social skills, who are the "life of the party," perhaps. The common thread is that these are all individuals who are highly regarded within their communities, and women are instinctively drawn to this. Other secondary factors include more generally masculine traits such as assertiveness, confidence, physical fitness, and the ability to provide for a family, of course.

The most critical thing to understand about sexual attraction as it pertains to our relationships is that no one controls their sexual desire, i.e. whether it arises in response to any given person; we can only control how it is acted upon, or not. These preferences are simply a force of nature which happens to us, or through us, and we have virtually no control over feeling or not feeling attracted to certain traits. Therefore, it is an absolutely fruitless waste of time to fight against them, to be frustrated, or blame the opposite sex for having these preferences. We simply must work with them, in whatever ways we can.

The next two chapters discuss how couples can deal with all of these opposing needs to have a harmonious partnership. Look at it as a list of suggestions, whatever doesn't work can be skipped over. Every person needs to go his or her own personal way. Once a person or a couple decides to make changes, supportive energies are freed up. The first step is the desire to want to make a change for the better.

CHAPTER 23

Taking Responsibility

"As much as I enjoy romance, it's commitment that I need the most. I need to know a love I can depend on, a love that says, 'I will be with you through it all. I love you. And I will love you even when you may not be all that lovable, for sometimes I'm not very lovable either. You can count on me - always.'" ~ Steve Goodier

IN THIS CHAPTER we discuss how to make decisions consciously, pondering the consequences before we make a decision, and once we make the decision, how to handle the consequences as they unfold, whether they adhere to our expectations or not.

The first thing to acknowledge is that we are responsible for the decisions we make in a relationship, including how we react to our partners, and also how we do or do not work with the forces of nature in the relationship. When we enter into a relationship, and especially when we choose to have children together, we are taking on a major responsibility, and this should be a part of our mindset, entering into it. We must go in knowing that a tremendous amount of work and even some sacrifice will be required to keep the relationship going beyond the seven-year mark, for the sake of the children.

The first step to making the right decisions is to understand the likely consequences of our actions, and that requires understanding the natural patterns discussed in the previous chapter, as well as understanding our particular partner through good communication. If a man refuses to discuss anything with his wife, for instance, knowing that she may need to process something verbally with him, or if a woman refuses to give a man any relief from the constant talking, in either case we are ignoring the needs of the other, and acting purely to satisfy our own desires without consideration of the consequences of our actions.

One of the most common ways people do this is by ignoring the requirements for sexual attractiveness, which sustains the sexual bond. Once married, a man may become lazy and complacent, not striving for any achievements or masculine strength, supportiveness, and self-determination which make him sexually appealing to his wife. Similarly, a woman may neglect the state of her physical body, throwing away the beauty and vitality which first drew her husband to her. In either such case, the partner is being careless and irresponsible in the relationship.

Let's break it down into facts: We know that sex is the primary bond and foundation of a romantic partnership. We also know that nobody controls whether or not they feel sexual attraction, including our partner. We likewise know that there are qualities we have some control over that make us more sexually appealing to our partner. Finally, we know that without maintaining the sexual bond the relationship is ultimately doomed, and that this inevitable separation will do great harm to the children.

Why, then, knowing these things, would we not strive to maintain these qualities, to keep the sexual bond alive, and the family together? The qualities our partners need for that attraction, after all, are good qualities to have. We would never be worse off for having a healthier body, or being more successful and proactive in life. There's really no reason not to put effort into this, other than simple laziness, ignorance of the facts, or unwillingness to take responsibility for our actions. This should always be a major priority, in every romantic partnership, though we all make mistakes and fall behind, at times.

On further reflection, it's even unethical to neglect this aspect of ourselves, because of the very nature of monogamy. If we are in a monogamous relationship, we have agreed to have the sexual bond with only this one person, on the basis that we have good chemistry with them, as well as the various other compatibility factors. If we then destroy that sexual chemistry out of our own neglect or laziness, yet we still demand sexual fidelity from the partner, we are essentially holding their sexuality hostage. We are saying that they cannot have a sexual life outside of us, yet we are refusing to provide what is necessary for an enjoyable sexual life with us, based on the instinctive preferences which neither of us have control over. This creates a terrible trap, with no good options for the partner, and is the underlying cause of many divorces.

The same principle applies to everything else we know about the nature of our relationships, including how the love shifts around between family members, and all of our partner's needs as a man or woman, and as an individual with their own unique preferences. Our concept of monogamy and it's responsibilities should always include an understanding of what is required for that relationship, ideally before we even enter into it. This is why knowledge of natural patterns in general, as well as communicating to understand our partner's particular needs are both critical.

With all of that being said, we must also acknowledge that both partners will at times fall short of this ideal, and make decisions which are not in the best interest of the relationship. Beyond taking responsibility for our actions, we must also react responsibly when our partner inevitably missteps, and this requires inner calm, and trust. It's said that in order to make a decision, one must trust themselves, and it's also said that people who trust themselves will tend to trust their partners. Trust is tantamount to a successful partnership. The problem is that most people don't trust themselves. This leads to questioning the very decision to enter the relationship, as soon as the going gets tough.

That's when they start to look for a new partner, hoping to find someone with whom they can live a simpler and better life. However, in reality, that's not how it works; people move from one relationship to another, and don't ever really commit, until they overcome this fundamental block. Simultaneously, each separation scars us, and we again try to avoid that pain in the future, leading to a diminishing trust in relationships in general, and an increasing difficulty in forming connections.

It is important to stick with our decision to be with our partner, in spite of seemingly insurmountable difficulties. It is more advantageous for people's happiness to push through these periods than to change the relationship on a regular basis. This is true even when there are no children. If everyone addressed their decisions in such a way, most relationship issues could be solved.

As soon as people accept this way of life, they can relax. The decision to accept our partner the way they are usually brings better results than to look for new and better relationships. Every time we end a relationship, something dies in us which reduces our capacity to love in the future.

The ability to trust, in spite of low self-esteem, is to stop looking at it as something external. We think we trust our partner because they behave in a certain way. The moment they disappoint us through their behavior, we look at it as broken trust, and the ship begins to sink. The entire dynamic described here is an illusion.

The actual trick is, to view trust as an internal decision instead of a factor to be affected by our partner. The decision to trust should come from within, with the intention to maintain it, no matter what our partner does. In reality, the most significant trust in our relationship lies not in the trust that our partner will behave appropriately, but in the Divine. We must trust that our relationship has a divine element, and that the obstacles which present themselves are meant to help us grow towards God, together.

Sounds difficult? It is, but with some effort even short of reaching an enlightened state of consciousness, it is attainable if we decide to live this way. The more we learn to tap into the unconditional love within, the less our ability to feel love depends on the other person and their behavior. When we really get the hang of this, we can simply be Love together, and face whatever obstacles come up together. We don't have to be enlightened to live with more love.

How do we do it, though? We all know the feeling of disappointment when our partner breaks a promise, hurts us, betrays us, or abuses us. The trick is that we decide at the beginning of the relationship, whether we can live with our partner, even if our worst nightmares came true. We need to consider the "what if" from the beginning and if our inner voice still says yes, then we decide to trust, with a certainty that this trust is free of any expectations from our partner, with an inner attitude inside of us to accept the other unconditionally, instead.

In order to maintain a relationship long-term, we have to decide from the start to accept the good and the bad, no matter whether expected or unforeseen.

The problem is that many think they are making that decision, but in reality, they are not. The number of separations these days speaks for itself. If everyone made those decisions in that way, there would not be any divorce. The problem with divorce is that it creates a vicious cycle, over generations. A divorce creates chaos not just for the parents, but even more-so for the children, and those wounds will tend to be passed on until someone breaks the pattern.

One needs to take the time to consider all possible consequences, and to accept them with all the suffering and difficulties that may arise. This is essential, if you are planning to have children. I cannot stress enough how important it is for the emotional and spiritual health of the children that the parents stay together until the children are grown up.

The only true solution to this problem is to trust that the relationship difficulties can be used for spiritual development, and that the love shared between you and your partner can overcome any challenge. Trust in the Divine and Unconditional Love is the key.

CHAPTER 24

Deciding On the Right Partner

"Give your hearts, but not into each other's keeping.
For only the hand of Life can contain your hearts.
And stand together yet not too near together:
For the pillars of the temple stand apart,
And the oak tree and the cypress grow not in each
other's shadow."
~Khalil Gibran

HOWEVER MUCH WE may intend to dwell in unconditional Love with our partners, the truth is that we will all fall short of that aspiration at least some of the time. Therefore, it's important to make the task of staying together easier and more likely, by being clear whether we can accept our partner's personality, as much as possible. Mutual acceptance is the basis for having children. When a couple has opposing views on life or personalities that are abrasive to one another, it will be difficult to respect each other. In this case, it is advisable to go and find a partner who you can have a harmonious relationship with, before a child is conceived.

There are certain factors that make it easier to live in mutual respect. Partners automatically have more understanding for each other if they live in the same kind of "world", meaning if their views on life and spirituality are the same. If they are very different in this way, life together can be difficult. This is not something that can be measured, but has to be intuitively felt out by each couple. It should be the chief thing on their mind, if they are considering a long-term child-bearing partnership. One must talk about the deepest subjects with a potential partner, to be sure.

Knowing compatibility also requires that we have clarity about what we want and how we want to live, for ourselves first. How can we know if the other person matches us, if we don't truly know ourselves? It goes without saying, then, that one must reflect on their own deepest desires for their life first and foremost. From there, it's a matter of assessing if the other person fits that pattern.

Professional recruiters are able to detect in 30 minutes whether an applicant will be able to perform well or not at a job. Even without those techniques we know after the second, third, or tenth encounter whether the other wants children, likes nature, or enjoys parties. After some months or years, we should know what they truly believe about life, and how they see the world and their place in it. We feel intuitively whether the person is a good fit, and through questions, we learn who the other person is, and their preferences, interests, and views on life.

There is no reason to try to change the other person, it's our own reactions to them which cause most of the trouble. If we can change our reactiveness, and learn to be happy regardless of their behavior, we can surmount almost any relationship difficulties. Knowing that we have an unlimited source of Love and peace within helps greatly in this; the bane of all relationships is the misconception that we depend on the other for our happiness.

Selecting a partner to start a family with is a matter of deeply understanding ourselves, the partner, our shared worldview, our differences, and how we can grow together.

A possessive mentality is another commonplace problem in relationships. We even take it for granted in such simple statements as: "This is my wife," or "This is my husband." It feels good to say this, even though it subtly turns the partner into property. Observe those around you with this type of mindset, and you'll see that they often treat their partner as property, eventually. When they get a new car, they are proud and treat it carefully. Every week they go to the carwash and check the oil and tire pressure. Then the car gets older. After a few years, it has dings, scratches and rust spots, and it doesn't get treated with the same care like when it was new.

The solution may sound strange to a society geared towards individualism, but instead of saying "You are mine," we might say, "I am yours."

The only way to keep love alive is to set our partner free, and this requires us to surrender our expectations and demands entirely. It's not easy, as all new skills are difficult to acquire. For a first grader, learning the ABCs seems to be an insurmountable obstacle at first, but most children manage it pretty quickly. The truth is that nothing in this universe is easy, but when we decide to learn something new, the right help and support will come to us to accomplish our goal. The process starts once we make a sincere decision.

As long as we are controlled by our fears and expectations, love cannot flow freely. Couples cling to one another because they are afraid to lose each other, because they think they need each other to feel love. When you understand that you can allow love to flow through you regardless of the partner, you no longer need to possess anyone. In a sense, you may no longer even need a partner, though you may still choose to have or remain with one.

CHAPTER 25

We Love Our Illusions

"I've looked at love from both sides now
From give and take and still somehow
It's love's illusions I recall
I really don't know love at all"
~Judy Collins

WHAT MAKES IT difficult for us to be freer in our relationships is the fact that we love our illusions. We want to live with them, even if we suffer because of them. Illusions can be beautiful, after all. In addition, we are accustomed to the suffering they bring. In the ups and downs between happiness and suffering, we find a strange sort of solace. Though it may be unpleasant, at least it's familiar. It's part of our nature.

People do not consciously look to suffer, but still enjoy it unconsciously, partly because they get attention as soon as they suffer and are sad. Friends, colleagues, neighbors feel sorry for them, and they enjoy it, unconsciously. When two people meet and start to exchange, they tend to speak about what isn't going well, rather than the beautiful moments of life. We don't feel safe enough to just be happy, since we cannot believe that we are entitled to lasting happiness. We lack trust in this condition, and knowledge that it is our essential nature.

People often don't realize until much later in life that a relationship brings both - downsides and upsides. You cannot have one without the other. Just as we all carry pleasant and unpleasant qualities within us, so do our partners. We want to remain in paradise and maintain the illusion that it will all be better with the next partner. This illusion is too nice to give up. It provides us with hope. It is much easier to think that if only the right man or woman comes along all will be well. It is much more difficult to explore what keeps us from living a fulfilled life.

Thus, we navigate between pleasure, hope, disappointment, and suffering, and repeat our relationship dramas over and over. At the beginning, we praise our partner as if they hung the sky, and later we put them down, oftentimes not realizing that we're simply a victim of our own projections. We are too often blind to the fact that the problem does not lie with the other person, but with us. Whatever place we are in today, we are the one responsible for it, whether through our actions in this life, or the karmic consequences of actions in past lives. We can't shift the blame away.

So how do we get out of this situation? Should we give up romantic love? Some choose to take up the monastic life, but there is another way for those who want to pursue a spiritual life and raise a family. It is to live and love and relate consciously, and to make it an aspect of our spiritual path. In Tantra, every aspect of our lives becomes spirituality, and romantic relationships and sex are certainly no exceptions.

The source of all our miseries is our fundamental misunderstanding of what love is. We think of love as a magical quality that somehow emerges when we meet the right person, or manage to find our way into a joyous moment. We wander through life, craving and chasing love, without ever actually stopping to truly understand it. Whatever the reasons that someone makes us feel it, what is this thing we're feeling.

The truth is that love is a shade of the light of our own true nature, the core of our being shining through. This is why we feel so alive and vibrant when we are in love, because it is bringing forward our true self, the same glorious thing which a spiritual teacher or a guru has the ability to bring out, but in a much more unconditional and transcendent way, in the latter case. Still, even romantic love offers us a glimmer of our own essence, and for many people who never encounter true spirituality, it may be the only glimmer they ever see. The trouble is all of the mental traps, assumptions, and illusions which we then unconsciously build up around it.

The chief illusion is that it isn't what we are, but something that comes to us only when we are with the partner. This is the source of all the addictive behaviors we display towards our romance. Indeed, if it were true that we only have access to our joyful essence through a partner, there would be good reason to be addicted. But of course, this isn't true. Even the unconditional Love of a spiritual teacher is only meant to guide us to this source of Love within, and a romantic partnership can be used for the same purpose, although it comes with many more traps and pitfalls, due to it's conditional nature.

This is also where trust comes in, because once we understand that love is just a limited glimpse of the treasure which lies beneath all of our illusions, even when it seems to "leave" us, when our partnership is unsatisfying, we can rest peacefully knowing that it is there, merely waiting to be freed from the illusions concealing it. It's only when we realize this that we need never worry or fret about our relationship ever again.

CHAPTER 26

The Fallacy of Believing We Can Know Another

"What a laugh, though. To think that one human being could ever really know another. You could get used to each other, get so habituated that you could speak their words right along with them, but you never know why other people said what they said or did what they did, because they never even know themselves. Nobody understands anybody." ~ Orson Scott Card, Shadow of the Hegemon

WE HAVE DISCUSSED the importance of communication and mutually attempting to understand one another for the health of our relationships, and it's true that we need to listen to each other, and consider the other's needs to inform our decisions. Couples need to make decisions that work for each individual, and that both can live with. This requires that they speak openly and honestly with each other.

The exchange between two partners should be one that fulfills the expectations of the other however possible, without sacrificing one's own fulfillment. It is about learning about the other, in order to develop a deeper understanding, and make appropriate compromises. However, it doesn't mean that either should be expected to agree to everything the other wants, or like everything the other thinks, feels, or does. Personal wishes and needs are equally important, and have the same right for existence. If you understand this you will adapt your demands, which in turn will facilitate life in a relationship. It's all about meeting one another halfway.

We want our partner to know us and understand us. Though we strive to understand each other, paradoxically, the truth is that no one can ever truly know the other completely. The sooner you accept this fact, the easier it will be to get along.

I have spoken to thousands of couples over the years and have experienced countless situations where I would learn facts about a relationship that were kept secret from the other partner. It is our desire that our partner knows us only the way we want him or her to know us, and this leads to us hiding parts of ourselves. Everyone has some things they bury so deep within themselves, only being on a spiritual journey can dig them out, or they may take them to their graves. It's best to simply accept this, and not worry too much about it.

The idea to know or understand the partner completely is pure wishful thinking. Whatever our partner will share with us we should receive, whatever he would like to keep a secret we should respect. The happiness of a relationship does not depend on how well you know each other. Rather, a relationship will gain immensely, if we accept our partner and allow them to set their boundaries as they see fit.

CHAPTER 27

Healthy Boundaries

"Your personal boundaries protect the inner core of your identity and your right to choices." ~ Gerard Manley Hopkins

WHATEVER IS IMPORTANT should be shared between partners, but this doesn't necessarily include things like details from a previous relationship, which could later be used in an argument against us. It's not always useful to include the partner in one's own inner processes, and this is particularly important for women. Often, it is better to discuss their issues with others, especially other women, than with their partner.

Women often think they can touch their partner with their tears, and this may work once or twice, but if it happens frequently, the man will get annoyed and retreat or withdraw. This only hurts the relationship, and the man will retreat internally, because men don't process things the same way that women do, by always "talking it out". Besides, it's an illusion to think that your partner can fully understand you. The only one who can really understand you is yourself, and even that feat may never be fully accomplished in your lifetime.

There is no danger in growing apart, if each follows their interests and preferences. On the contrary, the partnership will grow from it. When both follow their own path and figure out what they want to do, it can be together or separately, or probably both. The more freedom they grant each other, the more they can respect each other. It will not separate them. Partners who set their partners free and encourage them to stay true to themselves will receive more love, because then their Love is less conditional.

It's also best not to speak too much about work. When both partners come home it's advisable to close the chapter on work before we enter our mutual space. Our partners do not want to deal with the problems we encountered during the work day, or even if they do, it often only complicates things. What we all really want is to feel the relationship and enjoy each other in a playful way. It should be more about togetherness than the daily grind. Discussion of problems at work or about friends and family, should be kept to a minimum, even though those things need to be talked about at times. Your relationship should be a safe respite from these outer dilemmas.

The most successful marriages are those where partners don't spend too much time together, where they have some space. Relationships where one of the partners has to travel a lot, or couples don't see each other all of the time, are statistically more successful than couples who are always together. What counts is quality of togetherness, not quantity. We must each stand on our own, and when you spend more time apart, it makes the coming together all that much better.

CHAPTER 28

To Change Oneself

"Be the change that you wish to see in the world." ~
Mahatma Gandhi

IT RARELY HAPPENS that people will say: "I want to change for the sake of the relationship, so I will better fit my partner." This will even sound strange to some people, yet it is nevertheless helpful for a successful partnership. It's not about bending over backwards for the other person, but rather, part of the agreement of a romantic relationship should be to consider our needs and those of our partner equally.

If we want to be happy, it will behoove us to bring joy to the other person. If you give joy, you will receive joy. If you give love, you'll receive love. Love cannot be demanded. The focus should be on giving. As soon as we give, our partner will give back. It may take time to reprioritize for many people, since it's unusual to treat each other in this way. As soon as people embark on this path, the natural exchange of their partnership will start to flow.

The biggest problem is that we always want to get something back, and also tend to keep score on how much was given, vs how much was taken. It is difficult to surrender, and simply give. We typically give on the one hand, but expect something back. This will work for a while, but at some point, things will deteriorate, or tension will build until we explode.

How everything flowed so beautifully at first, we might think. We were curious about each other, we were there for each other, and were attentive to each other. Without realizing it, we crossed our boundaries. We gave more importance to the needs of the other than our own. We wanted to please them. We wanted to be loved. Somehow, we got caught in the spiral of adaptation. We bent over backwards, little by little, until we couldn't breathe anymore, and only wanted to leave.

Now, we have a choice. We can leave the relationship and our partner, or we can engage with them and look for new ways of acceptance, responsibility, and trust. As soon as we choose the latter, things will start to change. Through listening and talking to our partner, our love will reignite and the relationship can become harmonious.

CHAPTER 29

Dogmas in Our Society

"We are caged by our cultural programming. Culture is a mass hallucination, and when you step outside the mass hallucination you see it for what it's worth."
~Terrence McKenna

THE WALK ALONG the spiritual path is one that leads to more and more freedom, the further one goes, because it leads us to realize that the mental, emotional, and physical limitations, as presented to us through our education, our cultural understanding, and our social norms all lose importance. We learn that our perception of good and bad, as well as moral rules as they were given to us in childhood, are nothing more than guidelines on how to live together harmoniously as people. There is no real, objective significance to these rules beyond that.

The best gift that we can give ourselves is the gift of letting go.

When you are near enlightenment, you realize that there is no judging God who punishes us for bad behavior. There is no supernatural court that weighs our good and bad actions against each other. Karma is nothing more than our conviction that this reward and punishment exists. The conviction you hold at the time of death prevails and will reappear in your next life as a karmic remnant. When you are free of arbitrary conventions like the fear of being judged, or the hope of being rewarded, no

Karma remains that can catch up with us. On this basis, we don't need to discuss homosexuality, for instance, from a perspective in which the question of natural or unnatural is raised. From the perspective of the Source (God), everything is natural and all is one.

Karma, however, is not something you can simply think away with a mental decision, after reading the above lines. A person who feels guilty for something they did can try to convince themselves that it doesn't matter and push away the feeling of guilt. At the moment of death, they will still reconnect to these thoughts and take the energetic weight of this action into their next lives. Truly releasing Karma requires a deep inner spiritual process.

The old tantric teachings speak of four different Karmas. The first two are well known and are called good Karma and bad Karma. The binding principal is not the difference between these two Karmas; we can just as easily find ourselves entangled in the good Karma as in the bad Karma.

The lesser known third and fourth Karmas are called unattached Karma and attached Karma. These are more relevant to people on a spiritual path than the previous two. Attached Karma happens when we go through life and think we are the "Doer." That means we believe that everything that happens as a result of our decisions, good or bad, is actually done by us. When we are successful, it goes on our tally, and also when we fail. We might also push the blame on someone else. In this latter case, we are attached to the idea that the other person is the doer. Attached Karma is all about the illusion of Free Will, and the resultant judgement, praise and blame, rather than realizing that all human action is actually God's doing, in this play of illusion.

Unattached Karma occurs when we relinquish all responsibility of any result of our doings to the Source. That includes all good and bad deeds, all successes, and all failures. This, of course, is only possible if you relinquish the responsibility for both failures and successes. This can stem only from a state of consciousness where nothing actually comes from us, though it seems to from the perspective of duality. One who fully sees this disconnects entirely from the consequences of their deeds. If you still feel blame, doubt, and remorse, you know you haven't reached it. Yet, far from an excuse to be cruel or indulgent, this knowledge leads to liberation and all actions coming from a place of love, because all the obstructions to love are removed.

Also, if you feel pride, joy of victory, and success, you know you haven't arrived, since this is still being caught in the emotional entanglement of responsibility. Thoughts like "I did it, this was my success," are symptoms of this illusion. Only when you are free of all such assessments, you are living in unattached Karma. To live in unattached Karma is to no longer feel that you are a separate force influencing your life, but rather, you experience yourself as a witness to it. This is where freedom from the karmic cycle occurs, and though you continue living within the framework of actions and Karmas of all those around, you are free from it all.

Paradoxically, while we can recognize that only God is the doer, we will also continue living out the dream of doing and living, and therefore it's not a waste of time to attempt to act morally. When you realize your oneness with all beings, it's as absurd to harm another being as it would be for a finger to harm another finger on the same hand.

This contradiction between realizing that none of this chain of cause and effect belongs to you, and yet fully engaging with it, is a paradox that shows you are getting closer to truth, for truth is often paradoxical when expressed in dualistic language, and its framework of opposites. The key is that the "you" which you seem to be, the ego, is actually a part of this chain of cause and effect, and what you actually are is the Divine Consciousness behind it all, in a more absolute sense.

Karma results from and depends on our innermost belief systems and convictions.

CHAPTER 30

Sexual Preferences

"As a community, we should seek to create an environment that is inclusive of varying perspectives. Flat out, it makes us stronger. Diversity of thoughts and experiences opens us up to new ideas or to approaching old ideas in new ways." ~ Kevin A. Patterson

AS SOCIAL BEINGS, so much of our thoughts and behaviors are programmed by our social environment. One of the strongest areas of programming is our ideas about types of sexuality, like monogamy.

How upset we are when we find out, or even suspect that we may not be the only one for the partner. We feel betrayed, cheated, and deeply hurt. These attitudes have a purpose, since historically, it was socially advantageous to live in monogamy. To be monogamous means less sexually transmitted diseases, to minimize the transfer of energetic attachments, that fathers know who their children are, and so on. Without a doubt, monogamy brings many advantages, but the fact that this topic has been elevated to a moral authority is pure social conditioning.

The dogmatic assertion that we should live monogamously, that you lose face when your partner has sex with another partner, or that extra-marital sex is a sin, is based on conditioning. Feelings resulting from this conditioning are jealousy, embarrassment, and broken trust since the idea of eternal faithfulness was broken. All these feelings are natural to some degree, but are overly exacerbated by the strict application of rigid social rules governing our sexuality. I personally support monogamy as a way of life, only because I believe most people are happier in this frame, and since it solves issues of jealousy, sexual diseases, and avoids problematic energetic transfers.

The promise of eternal faithfulness and everlasting love, as well as the pain often resulting from it, is merely social programming.

There are societies that function very differently. In such societies, it is normal to change partners, and the feeling of jealousy is much more unusual. They learn from an early age that it is natural, and therefore do not get overly upset about it when it occurs.

The field of anthropology has shown us the degree to which this more lax view on sexuality and partners has been common among humanity throughout history. Lewis Morgan wrote in his book *Ancient Society* about the Iroquois of pre-colonial upstate New York, and describes how they lived in large family units, with overall equality of the sexes, and sexual practices based on Polyamory.

Similarly, Starkweather and Hames have found that the phenomenon of Polyandry (one woman marrying multiple men) exists today in 53 societies all over the world. Beckman and Valentine also observed the phenomena of divided fatherhood in several South American tribes in the Amazon, and they even prefer multiple inseminations at the time of conception, which is viewed as ideal. This also means that in some if not many cases, several fathers participate in a child's upbringing.

Then, you have the Mosuo in China, a people without shame regarding multiple sex partners. It is totally normal to have sex whenever and with whomever one wants. The children's education is handled by the mother and her relatives. There is no word for father. These are just some examples of how the way we see our world is decided by culture, and is not necessarily the only truth. Certainly monogamy is not ubiquitous, and before the conquest of European cultures and Abrahamic religions, alternatives were much more common than we typically think. Exactly how common they truly were, we may never know, so many cultures have come and gone.

I don't write these ideas to put down existing social norms; as I said, I support monogamy for most people. Still, this topic requires special attention. At least some of the people on this Earth have not been monogamous, and these practices have not proven disastrous for them. Yet, because of our culture, this is what is expected of our partners. It's clear that every romantic love has a shelf life; whether the relationship lasts in spite of this decline is another matter, but the romantic love reduces over time. Thus, some people in a partnership feel the need to satisfy the desire which their partner no longer satisfies.

There is no reason we should necessarily have to feel bad or guilty about seeking satisfaction elsewhere, so long as there is no deception involved. It seems that our society is not aware of this fact, and does not want to address it, nor account for it. Most people think that their love will last forever, and when this doesn't happen, they think there's something wrong with them. This assumption is incorrect, but results in a widespread belief that it is difficult to find a solution for the flood of divorces, and the resulting damage to children. As long as our society lives in this illusion and does not wake up to address this problem, we will not find a solution. Nature will run its course, we can only decide whether we allow it to do so peacefully, or we cause problems by attempting to obstruct its course.

Could couples, who would like to have children together, reach a point where they could openly assess their future development in terms of their sexual desires, and plan accordingly? Might they decide together to experiment with another couple? I don't want to say that this is necessary for all couples, but it is better than betrayal, breaking trust, and getting divorced over the disappointment of their eternal love failing, and damaging their kids' lives forever. Of course we have to watch out for the energetic transfer of negative energy here, which needs to be taken into consideration, and which we would be wise to protect ourselves from.

Can we culturally ask ourselves the following: Why does extra-marital sex hurt the partner so much? Why does it have to be done in secret, and is considered a betrayal? Why does it have to reflect negatively on one partner, if the other has a second partner? All these biases are programs that exist in our society and influence us. Any couple can discuss these things, move past them, experiment with other partners, and perhaps decide to give each other space. Then, in many cases it can be easier to live together, even beyond the seven years.

When both are able to be who they are, there is less reason to separate even after the love fades.

CHAPTER 31

Sexual Repression and Controversy

"When you express what is inside of you, that which you express will save you. When you don't express what is inside of you, then that which you don't express will destroy you." ~ The Gnostic Gospels

ONE OF THE great problems when it comes to sexuality are the many controversies which plague this area of our lives, and these are very often the result of repression or refusal to accept aspects of our sexuality which are natural. Therefore, I think it's worthwhile to comment on a few of these controversial topics, dispel some myths, and bring some things out of the darkness, into the light of spiritual insight and reason.

Here, I would like to discuss why homosexual or otherwise "non-traditional" relationships can take a very special place in spirituality. As we have learned, from a spiritual point of view, relationships that support love in an atmosphere of freedom are superior to relationships where love is connected to commitment. This has to do with the fact that this type of love has the potential to set our spirit free. It allows us to gain experiences, outside of the social convention of monogamy, the possessive mentality of relationships, and the conventional expectations of how to behave in our society.

Relationships in which you love in order to set the other free are superior to relationships in which you seek to bind the other.

I have noticed that homosexual relationships sometimes tend to display less of this binding factor, in comparison to heterosexual relationships. That doesn't mean that we should all look for same-sex partners, but we can take from these relationships an example of how sexuality can function without as much attachment. Please note that this is only a tendency, and it's also clear that there are examples in the heterosexual world where this is the case, and examples in the homosexual community where this is less prevalent. I'm just noting a common theme.

Generally, there is more and more acceptance of the LGBTQ community today, as well as the polyamorous way of life. As far as our society is concerned, this is a good sign, since the boundaries of personal preference become more tolerant and expansive, and the strict barriers of societal dogmas are weakening, step by step. This is progress.

Another topic I would like to just briefly mention here for clarification is sex during mensturation. In a 2015 poll of 500 people by The Flex, 55% of people surveyed were perfectly fine with sex while menstruating. At the end of the day, period sex is a personal preference, and it can be just as enjoyable as sex at any other time of the month.

Within sexual Tantra, menstruation is a powerful tool to elevate a person, and a couple. If the human woman were a plant, menstruation could be compared to the flowering of the plant. The spiritual power that can be derived from Tantra during menstruation is immense.

At the same time, we find various stigmas about this type of intercourse, that it may be dirty, unhealthy, or energetically damaging. That is only partly true. Of course, there is danger that always exists during intercourse, that negative energies are transferred by the partner, but this danger is independent of whether the partner is menstruating. Energetically, there is no difference pertaining to energetic transfer. However, there is a greater potential in terms of spiritual charge that can be achieved during this time.

The only things that count against intercourse during menstruation are a higher risk of the transfer of sexually transmitted diseases, and of course the cleanliness of one's sheets. In some Tantric practices, sex during menstruation is purposely used to harness certain powers. This is not a matter for this book, but at least we know that having sex during menstruation isn't harmful spiritually or energetically.

For people who are not working with sexual Tantra, it may be advisable to abstain during this time, since they do not derive any significant advantages, and a few disadvantages. However, if these minor problems are not a serious issue, there also isn't much reason not to have sex during menstruation.

On another note I would also like to briefly discuss age gaps between sexual partners. As long as the individuals engaging in a sexual relationship are both consenting adults, there is nothing intrinsically wrong with age gaps between partners. This is something which is increasingly judged in modern culture, in spite of the fact that it has been quite common throughout history. Some people have come to the mistaken conclusion that any relationship between an older and younger person, especially an older man with a younger woman, must necessarily mean that the older person is taking advantage of the younger person, somehow.

This is simply not true. People of differing ages come together for a variety of reasons, and to some extent it is natural for a woman to prefer an older man, and this is indeed often the case. Older people are often more competent, better able to provide for a family financially, and more mature. It's easy to see why this would be considered desirable by some people who are younger, and is not inherently harmful. If the two people love one another and engage in healthy relationship patterns, the age difference is inconsequential.

CHAPTER 32

Tantric Sexuality

"It's time we saw sex as the truly sacred art that it is. A deep meditation, a holy communion and a dance with the force of creation." ~ Marcus Allen

SEXUALITY IS ONE of the strongest desires we experience, as humans. We tend to think we know everything important about it, while in reality, sexuality is a very complex matter. Whatever we learn about it, we will discover new aspects, until we reach a Tantra level that is multi-orgasmic and without ejaculation. That means that men need to learn to ejaculate inside of themselves.

In the world of duality, love represents the female energy, and consciousness the male energy. Through intercourse, we enter the world of non-duality. Through the practice of Tantra, our Love is elevated to a spiritual plane. We become connected through our spirit, and not only through our bodies. Couples experience an unimagined depth in their relationship, and their quarrels lose importance, which helps them to stay together.

Normal sex is too often a quick and shallow undertaking, like a carpentar drilling a hole. In comparison, Tantric sex is very slow.

Physiologically men are weaker, even though they see themselves as stronger. They have more muscle mass, but they are not able to control their body as a woman can. As far as sexuality goes, women are much stronger.

Women need time to get aroused, men tend not to be able to hold their ejaculation long enough. When the woman barely opens up, the man is done. That is one of the biggest sexual problems in our time. The first step in solving this problem is that men recognize it as such, and start to work on solving it. As soon as men have developed an awareness of this, and are willing to work towards satisfying the woman completely, they will be able to learn a lot.

There are techniques, rituals, yogic exercises, even medical methods to keep the semen inside, and to delay ejaculation long enough, until both are fully satisfied. This will solve many problems. Psychologists can also play a part, because an early ejaculation oftentimes points to high performance expectations and goal orientation on achieving orgasm, as soon as an arousal happens. One can, for example, use an inner mantra as soon as the semen begins to rise, to calm the process.

It is all about slow sex, where the man excites his partner in a relaxed state. In this way, everything comes back to its natural order, old scars from unsatisfying experiences are healed. When a man treats the woman or even himself like a machine having mechanical sex, everything goes wrong.

Women have a very beautiful characteristic: when they are totally satisfied by their partner and feel totally fulfilled, they will generally not look elsewhere for other men. A woman who is interested in other men is probably not sexually fulfilled. We men should think about this fact. As soon as we recognize the problem, we are nearing the solution. As long as we are looking for weaknesses in the woman and asking her to adapt, we will not get anywhere.

The oldest problem with sex is that men and women have a different tempo. Men drive Porsches, and women like slow walks.

Here are a few suggestions for couples. Get creative, and already prior to intercourse, get intimate with each other. Slowly and gently indulge each other, engaging in long, drawn out, and mindful foreplay before intercourse.

Each sex has a primary skill which they must learn, in order to make progress in this regard. For men, it's important to learn Vejrauli, the ability to "injaculate." For women it is important to practice Shajauli, which is to strengthen and condition the pelvic floor.

For longlasting trantric sex, it is important that the man can stop his ejaculation. Ejaculation is oftentimes called "coming," while it is actually a "going." The man shares his life energy through the ejaculation, tremendous amounts of life potency in the semen, hormones, nutrients, and even a small amount of his personality. That is spiritually, mentally, and physically a huge sacrifice. Yet, among most, it is experienced as similar to the elimination of waste, with relief at being "empty" after.

During trantric sex, methods are used to maintain this energy, rather than losing it, and to engage in enjoyable sex without dissipating one's vital life force.

Exercises Prior to Intercourse:

- Alingana: Lovers embrace each other repeatedly. She may sit naked in the partners lap and wrap their legs around his waist.
- Chumbanam: Both kiss each other all over their bodies.
- Stana mardanadanam: The partners touch and kiss their torso and breasts.

- Dant karman:Lovers bite each other gently on the erogenous zones.
- Sparshanam: The body is touched gently and lovingly.
- Yoni Vistaran: The man awakens the Yoni (vulva) through gentle strokes and kisses.
- Lingam Pravesham: The man rubs the Lingam (phallus) on the Yoni until the woman invites him to enter.
- Mithuna: The Lingam is slowly inserted into the Yoni.
- Pravesham: The Lingam is inserted as deep as possible. It stays there for some time until the couple begins to move slowly.

CHAPTER 33

Tantra as a Way of Living in Harmonious Relationships

"The feeling of being alive and at One with everything is available through the path of Tantra. When your heart is open and you are making love, there is no separation between you, your partner and God. This is healing sex. This is connecting with the Divine. And the important thing to develop is the sense that this sacred experience is available in all instants. It is not limited to sex." ~ Philip Smith

TANTRA IS BOTH art and science combined, and supports people on their spiritual path to completion. Through its techniques, rituals, and spiritual practices, it helps fulfill and dissolve their needs, desires, and all that impedes them on their spiritual path.

Tantra reached the Western world, at a time when people had a particular desire for great sex, and so, they started to explore only a marginal area of the tantric path, the sexual area. They learned methods of fulfilled sexuality in order to improve their relationships. These methods, however, provide only a glimpse into the vast spectrum of Tantra.

Still, they are termed Tantra, or Neotantra. Therefore, the term Tantra, as it is typically used in the Western world, does not refer to the real, comprehensive path of Tantra, just as the term Yoga typically describes only some basic exercises, and not the complete philosophy and way of life which Yoga actually is. Likewise, in most people's minds in the West, Tantra only refers to the sexual component, which is a very small part of what this spiritual tradition truly is. True Tantra encompasses mantra, initiation, rituals, yoga, and meditation.

Tantra is a Sanskrit word and can be translated to mean simply "system." It is a system by which we can reach enlightenment, by which we can find the Divine Source, God or Goddess, and the knowledge of who we really are. It is a system that helps complete all aspects of life, and allows us to break free of all attachments.

There are many traditions in Tantra with varying orientations. All of them include these methods: Yoga, Mantra, meditation, energy transfer, fire rituals, sexual techniques, etc. The overall system is designed to be applied to every area of life, so that all of life can become a means to achieve enlightenment. A Tantra teacher supports each student individually with the appropriate methods, tailored to them.

Consummation, perfection, or completion of this path means that we don't need anything anymore. It doesn't mean that we don't need practical things for survival, but that we no longer desire anything, and whether or not we have any particular object of desire has no effect on our wellbeing. It simply doesn't matter anymore. We call individuals who have attained this condition permanently complete, self-realized, or enlightened.

Tantra assumes that a person is only free to embark on their spiritual path when they are free of needs and fears. This is why desires should be fulfilled. It would be nice if we could simply let go of our desires. That would be the best, but it does not happen through our intellect. It is possible to willfully abandon your desires, but if you are unsuccessful at doing so, you will find that they will come back at some point. It is then recommended that we fulfill our desires, in ways that will not harm anyone of course, so that they can naturally fade. We thus leave them behind, and can progress forward.

Letting go doesn't mean to make a decision to exclude something from your life. A man once said that he will stop smoking. During the three hours he spoke about it, he thought about tobacco at least 300 times. That is not letting go.

In the Indian tradition, the fulfillment of desires is not seen as a separate, materialistic part of life. It is an integral part of our development. Spirituality means fulfillment of all aspects of our lives. That is why we have so many rituals to support us in all areas of life, which are still being developed even today. Each master researches and observes precisely the results, and changes the details accordingly. It is therefore an ongoing, evolving tradition.

In the Tantric cosmology, the whole universe was created, and is imbued and maintained by two forces, which are intrinsically connected. These forces or universal aspects are called the divine male (Shiva), and the divine female (Shakti). In each man exists an inner woman, and in each woman exists an inner man. A woman consists of roughly 40 percent male and 60 percent female energy, and a man of 40 percent female and 60 percent male energy. In enlightened beings, this relationship is balanced to 50/50.

On the way to enlightenment, women acquire more masculine energy, and men acquire more feminine energy.

However, this alone is not all that is required for spiritual progress, but rather, is just a part of the process. Simply appearing more masculine as a woman, or more feminine as a man, is not equivalent to being more enlightened, as one can have very different ratios, and still be very entangled in Karma and various attachments.

CHAPTER 34

The Spiritual Teacher

"He who knows others is learned; He who knows himself is wise." ~Lao-tzu

HUMANS ARE EMOTIONAL beings, and because of a lack of skill in handling these emotions, usually we bounce back and forth between happiness and sadness. We worry about winning and losing, and get wrapped up in the duality of things. We spend inordinate amounts of our time worrying about the future, or are being busy with what happened in the past.

One of the things Tantra teaches us is to be in the "Here and Now," and not to worry about the past or the future. Most of our concerns are totally unnecessary, will most likely never occur, and have their origin in our various fears. That may be the fear to lose something or someone, or the fear of not being loved.

Tantra teaches us practices which propel us into a state of fearlessness, free of shame and hate, and leads us to a complete and blissful state. The first step is the initiation by an enlightened spiritual master, who transfers part of their energy through a large energy transfer (Shaktipat) to their student.

The master will then instruct the student to develop the energy that was transferred continually in themselves, to burn up fear, shame, and disgust within. They will guide the student to recognize divine energy in the moment, in all that is present, no matter whether it is considered good or bad. The master guides them past the contrast of duality to the Divine Source within them, so that they may feel and live their own divine potential.

Everyone who sincerely embarks on the Tantric path under the guidance of an enlightened master will sooner or later be free of shame, hate, and fear. Many believe that we can undergo this path without outside help. But if we think about it even for just a moment, we will find that almost everything in our life that we want to learn and understand fully requires guidance. Would you trust a plumber who had only read books about plumbing, or a surgeon who had only read Grey's Anatomy? Even in learning languages, we must at some point learn from a native speaker, to become fully fluent.

It is nearly impossible to reach Enlightenment without the help of an enlightened teacher.

When we are born, we are like a blank piece of paper. Our brain is like an empty harddrive, which we slowly fill with data, like language, behavioral patterns, and so on. This learning starts with our mother, who is our first teacher. Our father is our second teacher. The third teacher is our environment, where we derive knowledge from other family members, and books. The pedagogy in schools, universities and apprenticeship becomes the fourth. Some of us will also have a spiritual teacher, a fifth teacher that will provide us with the final, ultimate lesson. This final lesson involves unlearning all of the things we previously learned to function in society, as it is these very things which can hold us back from spiritual progress.

Our first four teachers help us learn what's necessary to live in society, but the fifth teaches us to let go of these ideas, in order to awaken the inner force of wisdom.

The statement that a master is needed on our spiritual path

is often met by resistance. There is a high degree of mistrust towards spiritual teachers. Many think that they are charlatans, make people dependent on them, and exploit them financially. Indeed, there are many examples supporting this claim. But maybe this mistrust also stems, to some extent, from the fact that spirituality is hard to grasp.

When our own intuition leads us to a spiritual teacher, we must only trust ourselves. We cannot expect positive feedback from outside when we speak of a Guru. The negative attitude towards spiritual teachers comes from the fact that many have slipped into the role to control, manipulate, and abuse people. Because many have done this, caution is warranted, but that doesn't dismiss the necessity of spiritual teachers.

I've spoken about various aspects of spiritual relationships. Our view of life, and our spiritual thinking and doing are a very personal and sensitive matter. It may be difficult to hear, but there are many false gurus in this world. Oftentimes it is those that appear particularly charismatic, since enlightened masters rarely project a large aura. They are not usually avid speakers, and prefer to remain unknown, which of course makes it even more difficult to find a true teacher. We can only rely on our intuition, destiny, or good Karma. It's not easy to determine who we can trust to guide us.

It is nevertheless a fact that a spiritual seeker needs a teacher, eventually. We make much progress through our many incarnations with little guidance, but we eventually reach a point in our evolution where we require proper instruction by one who knows from experience. There are many spiritual teachers at many different stages of development, and all have their purpose. A few have reached that state of complete unconditional loving existence which we seek, and can help others get there.

Spiritual matters are not unlike other complex areas, like engineering or medicine, in the sense that we cannot accomplish much on our own, though this might sound controversial. While religion has its place, many mistakenly believe that they need a priest, a church, or a temple to maintain a connection with God, and that they would be lost otherwise. Even today, most religions do not have it as their goal to lead people into independence. A true spiritual teacher, on the other hand, strives to "teach a man to fish," and help people have their own independent connection to God, rather than to "give a man a fish," and make people dependent on him or her.

You know you are on the right spiritual path, when it helps you feel more free, independent, and strong.

The difference between true and false gurus is that the enlightened Guru does not have a need to control others, or to maintain a certain appearance, himself. He or she will use the spiritual relationship to make the student stronger and more independent, so that one day they will become totally independent of the master. It is never about a church, a priest, or anything external. A true enlightened teacher will only help the student discover who they always were within, and help them develop all aspects of their being. As soon as we discover that God has always been within us, we will no longer need a teacher. This is what a true master does.

The internalization that we are God and that nothing exists outside of ourselves is the ultimate gift an enlightened master can give us.

It is at each person's discretion to find a spiritual teacher. Not every master is right for every person, just as not every person is right for every master. But when you find your enlightened teacher, you will realize that the teacher has no other goal than to help you reach a state of total independence and self realization. If that doesn't seem to be the case, you should be very cautious.

A good spiritual teacher will only lead their student to be more and more free, and not to be dependent on them.

CHAPTER 35

The Path to Completion Through Tantric Spiritual Practice

"We are not human beings having a spiritual experience. We are spiritual beings having a human experience." ~ *Pierre Teilhard de Chardin*

ALTHOUGH THIS BOOK is primarily about better relationships in normal life, because much of the advice given is from the Tantric perspective, I have included some general information here at the end pertaining to the path of Tantra, for any readers who are interested. Please note that fully embracing this path is not for everyone, and is not necessary for having happier and more loving relationships, but rather, is the path to spiritual realization for the few who are ready.

In the West, Tantra is seen as a purely sexual practice. In truth Tantra is a complete pathway, that includes many aspects that come together as a whole, with the goal of achieving wisdom. To take only one aspect of this path and leave the rest makes no sense, in the context of the path to enlightenment, and will surely miss the target. Below is a list of some of the most important areas of the Tantric path, which are designed to be practiced together like a harmonious orchestra in order to help the student advance in a transformational way.

The following chapters should only provide a glimpse into the tantric path, and are not meant as an instruction. The embarkation of the tantric path is only possible with the guidance of a master.

Initiation

Initiation is the foundation of a spiritual path. Through it, the assistance of the enlightened master acts as the medium between the Divine Source or Source power and the adept. Through this connection, the student's energy grows immensely, so that inner doors open automatically, and spiritual growth is enhanced.

Doubts towards a spiritual initiation are normal in our culture. Initiations are a very personal matter, and if any doubt exists in the adept, no initiation takes place.

An important aspect of initiation into the spiritual path is the shift of focus towards a new perspective on Love, which has nothing to do with the pursuit of happiness we normally think about in daily life. This new understanding involves striving for a state beyond the ups and downs of happiness and sadness, love and loss, or any inner state that's bound to the outer world. This alternate perspective on Love and happiness is ultimately for those who choose to fully embark upon the Tantric path, but this doesn't mean that striving to live a happy life isn't a worthwhile pursuit. From the perspective of a Tantric master, whether one chooses a more normal life, or that of a dedicated spiritual seeker, ultimately makes no difference.

Meditation

Meditation is an important practice in the process of letting go. Anybody who finds themselves on a spiritual path, whether they feel all-in or just testing the waters, changes every moment. He or she will go further within, and this process changes their demands on life organically.

First, you have to perfect your physical and mental abilities, and then learn to control, refine, transform, and divert them, in order to bring the soul to a higher plane of spiritual development. This allows you to control your anger, hunger, thirst, hate, ego, and to perfect concentration, psychic abilities, and sexuality.

The goal of meditation is to eliminate the fixation on the senses, to orient the mind, and look inward. It is a retreat from everything we sense through sight, smell, hearing, taste, and touch.

If you are disturbed by outer sounds when you meditate, you have not reached a true meditative state.

In order to retreat successfully from your senses, it is important to improve your ability to concentrate. This is called "Dharana" in Sanskrit, which means "focused concentration." Dharana prepares us for deeper states of meditation. We concentrate on an object of meditation, or imagine total darkness. This depends on your individual path, which may pass through duality or non-duality.

For a spiritual teacher, it does not matter if someone takes the path of duality or non-duality, he meets the person wherever they are.

We reach a point where we are so focused that we do not perceive anything but the object of our meditation. A person who does not focus on an object should see only darkness with their inner eye. When we master that, we speak of meditation. Before that, we say we meditate, while only sitting with eyes closed. In this state, we begin to understand what meditation really is. We perceive wisdom, and an understanding of the true nature of bliss, and what it can mean for us.

A meditative state is reached when the external world disappears, when we do not hear or see anything anymore, and everything happens only inside.

This state of deep meditation is called the state of nothingness. We do not perceive anything from the external world and are fully immersed in our innermost reality. This state cannot be fully described in words, but can only be experienced subjectively.

Yoga

Balanced relationships need a healthy body, and a very healthy mind. That includes partnerships, as well as familial relationships and friendships.

Yoga leads us through a cleansing process, and strengthens various aspects of our beings. Body and mind are cooled down energetically, which helps us to let emotions like anger or sadness to flow through us and out of us, without being influenced by them.

Tantra yoga includes the external cleansing, the inner cleansing, physical exercises, breathing exercises, and meditation.

Aspects of the outer cleansing are the love for truth, a life of nonviolence, no stealing or hoarding of things, and the mindful use of sexual energy. When you follow this way of life, you will experience a deeper harmony in your relationships. The environment has less influence on our own wellbeing, and we therefore experience less negative feelings typically caused by lack and neediness.

The inner cleansing process includes a clean body, a simple life, self discipline, the release of desires, self inquiry, and the study of the spiritual master's teachings. The inner cleansing culminates in the total surrender to the Divine Source. This requires that we master all aspects, and integrate them into our lives.

The physical exercises of yoga, so-called Asanas, strengthen the body. If you visit our meditation center (Ashram) in India, for instance, you will learn a harmonious sequence of Asanas. The full sequence takes 30 to 45 minutes. At the end, you'll typically say a short prayer, with which we bow and thank our mother, our father, our spiritual master, all planets, all Goddesses and Gods, and all those who have given us energy and support us. The prayer ends with a plea for peace in our environment, and the entire universe.

The daily practice makes the body flexible and limber, and we can sit with crossed legs as long as necessary, in order to practice multiple hours of Tantra as advanced students. In general, however, there are no rules as to which Asanas one should practice. You can choose your own Asanas, and slowly start this physical aspect of your practice.

Couples can also practice partner yoga. These exercises bring us to a higher spiritual plane and facilitate conversations in the relationship. They strengthen the trust in each other, and help us speak to our partner about our feelings.

Breathing Exercises

Breath is the source of life, and breathing exercises (Pranayama) help us to strengthen certain mental and energetic abilities in our body. The goal is to liberate the breath. Through these techniques, the mind becomes quiet, so that we can concentrate more effectively. Pranayama also has a harmonizing effect on our emotions and supports digestion.

These five exercises work well in the beginning: Nadi Sodhana (alternating breath), Kapalbhati (Breath of Fire), Bhastrika, Bhramari (Bee's breath) and Sahita Pranayama. With time, you can expand to explore more breathing techniques. Couples can also exercise all Pranayama methods together, and synchronize their breath during the exercises.

When you do Pranayama together, you should perform the exercises with a certain consciousness and intention. This way, you can inhale, burn, and exhale negative thoughts, feelings, and energies with each breath. Pranayama helps to leave behind quarrels and misunderstandings in the partnership, and to open a path for loving togetherness.

I believe that you don't need more than the above to keep a relationship healthy, unless you want to find out more about your emotional entanglements and find ways to break free. For those who seek a deeper understanding and want to embark on the path of enlightenment For those who seek a deeper understanding and want to embark on the path of enlightenment, you may want to contact us for more information regarding our annual 8 day India retreat exclusive for those interested in the path of enlightenment and our various retreats around the world.

Enlightenment

Other terms for Enlightenment are individuation, self realization, spiritual perfection, bliss, or Samadhi in Sanskrit. This condition has nothing to do with what most people believe it to be. Most people think bliss is a form of extreme joy. But being truly enlightened has nothing to do with joy. The meaning of Samadhi relates to the ability to see all things as the same, and without distraction by our thoughts. In this state we experience neither likes nor dislikes. We lose the desire to evaluate and judge. It is a condition in which we no longer experience joy or sorrow, in which we experience bliss. We remain calm and even-minded in all situations, and will not get distracted by emotions. We feel, but our feelings don't influence our actions.

The spiritual path means leaving the ocean's surface, full of ripples and waves, to enter a deeper water of absolute stillness.

Printed in the United States
By Bookmasters